# LOST
## LAKE CHARLES

# LOST
## LAKE CHARLES

**ADLEY CORMIER**

THE History PRESS

Published by The History Press
Charleston, SC
www.historypress.net

Copyright © 2017 by Adley John Cormier
All rights reserved

*Front cover*: courtesy McNeese University Archives.
*Back cover*: courtesy McNeese University Archives.

First published 2017

Manufactured in the United States

ISBN 9781625858825

Library of Congress Control Number: 2017934926

*Notice*: The information in this book is true and complete to the best of our knowledge. It is offered without guarantee on the part of the author or The History Press. The author and The History Press disclaim all liability in connection with the use of this book.

All rights reserved. No part of this book may be reproduced or transmitted in any form whatsoever without prior written permission from the publisher except in the case of brief quotations embodied in critical articles and reviews.

Lost Lake Charles *is dedicated to Melinda Antoon Cormier, a woman of infinite creativity and boundless patience.*

# CONTENTS

Acknowledgements 9
Prologue 11
Preface 13

1. The Early Days 27
2. Crafting a City 39
3. Ingredients for Growth 49
4. The Great Fire 75
5. The Twentieth Century 87
6. Crafting a Future 103

Appendix: How to Discover History on Your Doorstep 131
Bibliography 137
Index 139
About the Author 143

# ACKNOWLEDGEMENTS

Many sources were used for the research and writing of this book. While there are very few published academic histories of Lake Charles, there are literally hundreds of unpublished theses, newspaper and magazine articles and monographs on elements of Lake Charles history available at McNeese State University Frazar Library Archives and Special Collections, including the copious scrapbooks of Maude Reid, which provide a personal commentary on popular history, and the collections of the Calcasieu Parish Library at its Southwest Louisiana Genealogical and Historical Library branch at the Carnegie building in downtown Lake Charles.

In producing this book, the author acknowledges the additional research and the work, both published and not published (or now out of print) of the following historians and journalists: Lloyd Barras, Jim Beam, Robert Benoit, W.T. Block, Mark T. Carleton, E. Harper Charlton, Edwin Adams Davis, Stewart Alfred Ferguson, Louis C. Hennick, Mike Jones, Don Kingery, Donald Millet, Maude Reid, Nola Mae Ross, Ward "Buddy" Threatt, Joe Gray Taylor, Thomas Watson and T. Harry Williams.

Special acknowledgement is made to the archives of the *Lake Charles American Press*, whose online access of Lake Charles newspapers is complete to 1898.

Special acknowledgement goes to McNeese State University Archives and Special Collections at Frazar Memorial Library, and to Pati Threatt,

# Acknowledgements

archivist, for access to theses, scrapbooks, notes and reports, as well as for images as noted.

I want to give special acknowledgement to Imperial Calcasieu Museum executive director Susan Reed and curator Devin Morgan for images as noted.

Information about National Register of Historic Places properties, processes and nominations is from the websites of the National Register and from that of the Louisiana Department of Culture, Recreation and Tourism.

Information about programs of the Calcasieu Historical Preservation Society (CHPS) is from the society's website and from minutes of the society.

Information about Louisiana Speaks, the Downtown Development Authority and the Historic Preservation Commission of the City of Lake Charles is from the minutes of the authority and the commission.

# PROLOGUE

The best way to tell a story is to tell the whole story. To do that, you sometimes have to use props and pictures, offering evidence to prove a point more quickly and make that point more clearly. Actual, existing buildings make it easier to tell the whole truth when it comes to telling local history, which is, of course, the whole truth of a place.

A 1920s view of palm-lined Broad Street, with the Kirkman streetcar in the middle ground. *Courtesy McNeese University Archives.*

# Prologue

In Lake Charles, Louisiana, a central fact of its history is that at one time there were lumber mills that processed pine and cypress. There is no tangible evidence of that great sawmill industry today—you just have to imagine the mills on the shores and the logs floating on the water, the steam-powered saws ripping three-hundred-year-old cypress into boards around the clock. You certainly can't smell the sawdust and you can't sense the steam. In fact, the only legacy of the industry that you can actually see today are the many Victorian and Edwardian homes built from that very cypress and pine.

Another central fact is that for over thirty years a progressive Lake Charles had streetcars that served the entire community and operated around the clock! There is no evidence of that today. Gone also are the sailing schooners, the edges of lakes and waterways dark with cypress and tupelo loaded with Spanish moss, the ferry landings of the *Rex* and the *Hazel* and even the railroad stations that once tied this community to the world. Visual testaments of a rowdy and colorful past are all gone—and now nearly forgotten.

This book will help you remember a history that you may never have known.

# PREFACE

## Who and What We Are

In terms of Louisiana history, Lake Charles is a relatively young city. Natchitoches and New Orleans—and more than a few other Louisiana cities and towns—have a 100- to 150-year head start. But even taking that into consideration, Lake Charles has a colorful, complex and diverse history in many ways different from other communities in the state. For much of its existence, Lake Charles's story is perhaps more typical of that of the boom-and-bust American Wild West than that of the sleepy Deep South. The threads of distance and isolation, of independent action taken in the face of adversity and of ready access to the wild and the open may have colored the history of Lake Charles like no other city in the South.

Intrepid early pioneers developed a self-reliant culture of cattle grazing, subsistence farming, hunting and fishing rather than that of agrarian indigo, cotton or sugarcane plantations that was the standard pattern in the rest of Louisiana and in most of the South. With newcomers to the southwest Louisiana area, the cutting and processing of lumber became another source of wealth, followed in time by rice; by extractive industries like sulfur and oil; by transportation, refining and petrochemicals; and even by aviation. As soon as the area was connected by rail to the rest of America, the once isolated southwest Louisiana became the unique focus of one of the earliest large-scale land promotion

## Preface

The wild and lonely shores of Lake Charles can well be imagined from this image taken in the second half of the nineteenth century. *Courtesy the Imperial Calcasieu Museum.*

schemes in North America. The search for an open and honest history that explores the untold and sometimes quirky saga of this corner of Louisiana is the purpose of this book.

## A Place of Neighborhoods and Small Villages

Lake Charles is a place of neighborhoods and small villages. In city planning jargon, the map of the city reflects that of a "poly-centered net," which means that there are multiple areas of community and civic focus scattered over a network of streets and roads. While some neighborhoods serve as places to live, others focus on retail, industry and business, hospitality and casinos, education, healthcare or government. As the city grew from its start on the lake, the direction of growth has been generally southward and toward the east, and now that growth has literally jumped over the Calcasieu River and English Bayou on the north, there is poly-centered growth in the Moss Bluff and Gillis areas, once viewed as the remote countryside.

Many neighborhoods and villages, that is to say districts made up of several neighborhoods, have changed over time from residential to commercial. Sometimes, change is the result of the unique geography of the area, perhaps a new business project, new highway or waterway opening up fresh opportunities and eliminating others. Occasionally, change comes from adjustments in society or in the economy. And, of course, so near to the coast, change can be caused by natural disaster, as a result of climate modification or even by rezoning for elevation requirements.

The now linked Downtown/Lakefront is both the oldest and perhaps the most changed and most changeable of all the city's "villages." The waterfront itself was once a place of industry, warehousing and transportation with a mixed-use commercial downtown about two blocks inland to the east. The historic waterfront was the site of warehouses, rail spurs, sawmills and ferry landings, and the downtown core was for professional offices, retail, government services, restaurants and hotels. Downtown/Lakefront today offers a distinct, updated identity for Lake Charles. Many social, fundraising and cultural events are scheduled at its well-recognized landmarks. It's where most visitors and many locals identify as the living room of the region.

This midcentury view of the lakefront and downtown, taken from about the center of the lake, shows the close relationship between land and water. Water—either river or lake—borders the entire northern and western edges of the city. *Courtesy the Imperial Calcasieu Museum.*

## Preface

There is a separate civic authority to monitor and encourage growth for the area, the Downtown Development Authority (DDA) of the City of Lake Charles. The DDA encouraged the merging of what had been viewed as separate parts of the city and even today tries to eliminate the public psychological division between the two. Spurred by Hurricane Rita damage, DDA projects literally reshaped both the water's edge and Ryan Street as part of general storm recovery. With the support of the mayor and the Lake Charles City Council, the DDA today continues to prepare and shape the area for development. Downtown/Lakefront has become the entire region's showcase and playground, with new and engaging activities scheduled there, including seasonal festivals and fairs. Many new recreational and social venues, galleries, banking, apartments, retail, restaurants and professional offices are now in operation. It's an area that both works and plays today.

The Victorian-era Charpentier District, roughly from Belden Street on the north to Iris on the south, and from Hodges Street to Louisiana Avenue, is a National Register historic district. The Charpentier District honors the mostly French-speaking carpenters who constructed its collection of over four hundred period structures over roughly fifty years beginning in the 1870s. The district has some commercial and professional offices along Broad Street and Kirkman Street, but principally, it is residential in nature. At almost fifty blocks, the Charpentier National Register District is rather large, and it is made up of many different neighborhoods. As a whole, it is connected by its heritage of wooden architecture. Many of the buildings were constructed using the cypress and pine once harvested and processed in the city. The district, like most historic districts, connects us visually and viscerally with the past by its preserved historical inventory of structures.

Other historic areas include Margaret Place, a jewel box–sized city historic district that features bungalow and other construction from the early part of the twentieth century. Another is Baptist Meadows, a collection of neighborhoods dating from roughly 1910 to 1970 with a range of house types, sizes and shapes. Named for the now-lost Louisiana Baptist Orphanage, an early landmark of that part of the community, Baptist Meadows is south of the Charpentier District and east of Margaret Place. To the east and southeast of Baptist Meadows is the manicured neighborhood of Edgemont, clustered near the site of the historic Lake Charles High School and to the south. Edgemont features many properties from the 1930s through the '60s and has some stellar examples of midcentury design. Even farther east and south, the planned Oak Park district has homes from the 1940s through the 1980s and is the very definition of shaded, suburban tranquility.

PREFACE

The Charpentier District includes over four hundred structures on about fifty blocks. While many homes are grand, like this one, there are also great examples of cottages in a variety of sizes and shapes. *From the author's collection.*

On the northern edge of the city, bound by the upper Calcasieu River and English Bayou, Goosport, established by early German settlers, was once a complete town on its own with sawmills, shipyards, shops and homes. Today, it has converted to being mostly residential but still offers a freshwater riverfront ready for reuse with a few industrial and commercial sites here and there. Fisherville, to the west of the intersection of busy commercial Highway 90 and US Highway 171, and Deesport, centered on Contraband Bayou, began as residential areas for working men and women. Each area flirted with some industrial and commercial activities in the early part of the twentieth century; today, both are ripe for redevelopment. In the east and southeast edges of the city are Broadmoor, Greinwich Terrace and Greinwich Village, designed to provide essential housing during the industrial boom and military expansion from the 1940s to the '60s. These areas have seen social and economic changes, both up and down, with pressures caused by commercial activity on its edges. There are many other neighborhoods and villages, some with firm identities like named subdivisions and others that identify with schools or local churches or other landmarks.

The roadways and streets that connect these villages and neighborhoods mostly change as the neighborhoods themselves change, but some streets do have characteristics of their own—they are long, thin neighborhoods of a sort. The historic commercial and business corridors of Railroad Avenue, Broad Street, Prien Lake Road, Martin Luther King Highway, Gerstner Memorial and venerable Ryan Street are currently being supplemented by Lake Street, McNeese Street, Sale Road, Ihles Road, Nelson Road and other thoroughfares being created or entirely reconfigured in south Lake Charles. In fact, the entire concept of south Lake Charles is relatively new, with many neighborhoods identifying as such having been created only in the last ten years or so. As the city limits move southward, the definition of where south Lake Charles starts depends on whom you ask, with longtime residents pegging the northern edge variously at Twelfth Street, Eighteenth Street, Prien Lake Road, Sale Road or McNeese Street. The younger the resident asked, the more southerly the boundary offered as an answer.

However, the real move southward began more than a century ago with the establishment of the Lake Charles Country Club at Prien Lake. A southward focus was encouraged and reinforced by the construction of Barbe High School at the western end of McNeese Street in the early 1970s. Alfred M. Barbe High School, named for a member of a pioneer family, served as a natural crosstown rival both to Lake Charles High (established in the 1890s on Enterprise Boulevard) and to the 1950s LaGrange High (on Louisiana Avenue).

Since the watershed year of 2005, when Louisiana was visited by Hurricanes Katrina and Rita, the shape and future of Lake Charles and, frankly, that of the entire Gulf Coast, has been publicly examined in terms of how best to develop and grow in an area so delicately positioned on the edges of water and land. For some, available real estate in south Lake Charles or in Moss Bluff offers opportunities for growth in a strictly traditional suburban fashion, but only to the point determined by distance from services and elevation above mean sea level. For other, perhaps more discerning developers, the creative reuse of vacant or underused land within the traditional city boundaries offers bountiful opportunities for innovative projects that are land-conscious, that is, sensitive to the concept of sustainability with smart, tech- and earth-savvy development.

Several post-Rita recovery projects underway are particularly land-conscious. The developers are sensitive of wisely using existing high land or to create sustainable, buildable land and extract as much value as possible from it. This means building with tested materials to higher construction standards, as well as building at higher base-level elevations to reduce the effect of wind and storm surge. Economic viability is directly challenged by the higher costs of sustainable development and by the actual unique geography of the area.

Post-Rita developments include the Walnut Grove community, a new-urbanist project that uses a portion of what had long been viewed as marginal swampy land east of the City Docks and south of Sallier Street. Completely land-farmed, the property was elevated significantly and made suitable for a mixed-use community being built from scratch. The Graywood development southwest of Lake Charles has aspects that are land-conscious with broad bands of green space and water courses in lower areas and clusters of residences at higher elevations. It's very sensitive to watershed, drainage and access.

More modest in scale are various new townhouse projects that provide fresh urban living options, even though some are being built in suburban neighborhoods. Townhouses, compact and spare in terms of land, are in stark contrast to the traditional suburban models that offer expansive lawns and lots of space between residences. Two notable townhouse examples exist close to downtown. The first, just north of Pithon Coulee in what had long been viewed as marginal land, is a complex of traditional-looking townhouses built on a freshly elevated and reinforced topography. The second is a row-house development modeled on Lake Charles–style wooden houses and constructed on a high but long-vacant half-block lot between the traditional downtown and the Charpentier Historic District.

Other significant projects that rethink the post–World War II suburban sprawl model include Morganfield, being developed in southeast Lake Charles. This will use the new-urbanist template of walkable mixed-use centers and another is a planned upscale apartment complex with urban amenities like stacked accessible parking (but reflecting traditional exteriors).

# Preface

Hurricanes have played a part in shaping Lake Charles. Here, the effects of the 1918 storm can be seen on Ryan Street. *Courtesy McNeese University Archives.*

This project is breaking ground on the now remediated site of the demolished city block–large Sears retail store in downtown Lake Charles.

In the 150-year history of the City of Lake Charles, there has been a thread of generally good stewardship of resources, on both a private and a civic scale. While much of that stewardship derives from a long-held conservative approach to most issues (certainly politics, financial and commercial ventures), a substantial part of that stewardship was an early realization of the limits of the physical geography. High ground is a valued resource in coastal Louisiana, and transportation connections are essential for growth and development. Engaged human capital, that is to say, knowledge and know-how, is the key on how best to manage the two.

To some extent, *Lost Lake Charles* is the story of the degrees of stewardship and how to best use the resources at hand. What has happened and why, the lessons learned from experience and the interconnected changes wrought from those decisions make for a fascinating, complex and sometimes apparently contradictory read. If nothing else, the story of Lake Charles is a

# Preface

microcosm of what it means to be a city, building and changing and growing itself perched on a watery plain on the edge of the continent.

Lake Charles serves as the principal urban area of the entire southwestern corner of Louisiana, a region of nearly ten thousand square miles of prairies, marsh, woodland and open water. Not only is Lake Charles the control center that provides access and management of the resources of this region—the center for retail, commercial, educational and hospitality ventures—it's also home to nearly 100,000 people within the city and its suburbs. Yet it is surrounded by millions of acres of near-wilderness, sparsely populated and home to herons, egrets, alligators and other wildlife.

The various names of longtime Lake Charles families suggest a rich tapestry of origins. A few Native Americans were assimilated into pioneer settler families. Early settlers included Creoles and African Americans. The French- and Spanish-speaking families here welcomed Americans from Georgia, the Carolinas, Kentucky and Tennessee after the War of 1812. As part of the North American pattern of immigration, southwest Louisiana welcomed Germans and other northern and western Europeans prior to the Civil War. After the war, Michigan Men (known elsewhere in the South as

Many early leaders of the city can be seen in this 1920s image of the Masons at the Hodges Street lodge, which preceded the impressive Masonic temple that stands there now. *Courtesy McNeese University Archive.*

carpetbaggers), midwesterners and eastern and southern Europeans sought opportunity in Lake Charles. With the discovery of oil and the growth of the military, education, medical services and petrochemical and related industries, new neighborhoods here include Latin Americans, Asians and Middle Easterners.

Lake Charles is part of the global economy. The port and the industries are an important factor in globalization, and the university and community college support that economy. Faces you see on the streets, in the cafés and in the supermarkets are from throughout the world.

## Geography and Topography

The southwest corner of Louisiana is part of the Gulf coastal plain and comprises some of the youngest land on the North American continent. Young land on the southern edge of a great continent, our home was also the last part of Louisiana to have been settled by Europeans and by early Americans.

The City of Lake Charles is physically located on the eastern shore of the Calcasieu River, about thirty miles north of the Gulf of Mexico. The namesake body of water is a widened outflow of the river—roughly one and a half miles square. The Calcasieu River, while not particularly long, drains much of southwest Louisiana and, on its lower half, sports a number of brackish, lagoon-like lakes along its course. Just north of the river's mouth on the Gulf is the largest, Calcasieu Lake, or, as it is more popularly known, Big Lake. Strung along the river moving northward are Moss Lake, Prien Lake, Indian Bay and, finally, Lake Charles, the actual body of water that forms the western edge of downtown Lake Charles. These lakes and the now-channelized and regulated lower Calcasieu River are vital to the productivity and economy of the region.

Man-made changes in the lower Calcasieu converted what had been a sluggish, winding bayou with sandbars and a dangerous undertow into an efficient instrument of transportation and industrialization. These changes were crafted largely through the efforts of the Port of Lake Charles, which serves as a hub of rail, pipeline, highway, barge and oceangoing traffic. Nearly 120 years of engineered changes to the surface of the land and to area waterways have been responsible for the impressive industrial and commercial growth of the area. This morphing of the topography is also proving to be a threat in time of storm or flood.

# Preface

Just to the south, flat prairie land changes to freshwater and then to saltwater marshes that provide habitat for wildlife. This is an image of the appropriately named Calcasieu Prairie National Wildlife Refuge. *From the author's collection.*

While most of Lake Charles is not even twenty feet above mean sea level, it is at the apex of three distinctive landforms. To the south are marshes, freshwater and, closer to the Gulf, saltwater that provide habitat for wildlife and nurseries for marine life. To the east and southeast are the flat grasslands of the Calcasieu prairie, now planted with rice, soybeans and sugarcane and serving as grazing for cattle. To the west and north, bands of pine and mixed hardwood forests merge into the Big Thicket of east Texas and connect with managed pinelands to the north, respectively. A ten-minute drive from downtown Lake Charles south, east, west or north reveals entirely different vistas—landscapes that helped to shape Lake Charles's colorful history.

From a modest beginning as an isolated community on the shoreline of a remote stream, Lake Charles built on its unique geography and natural resources by connecting those elements to a larger world market. The development of resources (cattle, timber, agriculture, sulfur, oil and gas) was interconnected with improvements in transportation (sail, rail, roadways, pipeline, and maritime, from inland barge to oceangoing vessels). The city was built on its resources and the methods these resources got to market.

Having no bedrock (no rock at all to speak of) on which to build, and with a surface area of malleable marsh, prairie, woodland and open water, Lake Charles has seen major alterations and changes to its physical appearance in its 150-year history. Man has cut canals, drained marshes, cut over timberland, raised fill and altered watercourses. Add the occasional flood, hurricane and fire, and the man-made environment of the Lake Area has been in a state of near-constant flux from the day of its first settlement.

No truer city biography can be crafted than that of an earnest examination of its now-bygone landmarks and of its nearly forgotten heritage. In the rush toward a unified world where many products,

# Preface

Early roadways like the Old Spanish Trail followed Indian trails and the routes of the seasonal cattle drives that crossed the area from west to east. *Courtesy McNeese University Archives.*

buildings and movements are uniform commodities, local heritage retains the spice of innovation and the seasoning of diversity, certainly in meeting local needs and creating a local identity.

Many current architectural versions of structures, for example, are the second, third or even fourth editions of a lost original, with each version meeting the needs at the time for which it was constructed. In some cases, the original edifice is gone forever. Some landmarks (and the history they represent) were erased for necessary new improvements. Others succumbed to neglect, bad judgment or bad luck. To visit and explore the evidence of Lake Charles's history and how that history was lost (or changed) is the purpose of this book.

# 1
# THE EARLY DAYS

## THE ISHAK

The earliest inhabitants of what was to become Lake Charles were roaming bands of Ishak Indians. Much of what we know about the Ishak came from what now appear to be biased accounts from other Native American tribes at the time. The neighboring tribes, the Chitimacha and the Natchez, warned the first French and Spanish settlers that the local tribes were cannibalistic and renegade. Even the name by which the native inhabitants are perhaps better known, Attakapas, is actually the Chitimacha tribal word for "man-eater" and not an Ishak word at all. As the European explorers first encountered the Chitimacha and their advanced native culture, those same explorers adopted and used the Chitimacha term for the neighboring native peoples and, to some extent, adopted the derisive attitude about their nature and character. The Ishak were essentially handicapped by bad press even before contact with the white man.

The range of the Sunrise Ishak covered most of southwest Louisiana. One of the earliest French garrisons in Louisiana, Poste des Attakapas (now St. Martinville), marked the eastern edge of their traditional range. The Sunrise people were part of the greater Ishak people that had two components: the Sunrise people east of the Sabine River and the Sunset people west of the Sabine. While linguistically connected to the western and southern plains Indians, and possibly even to the Aztecs, the Ishak were remote from their

Traditional Ishak trails provided access through grasslands and woodlands in pre-European times and were used as a part of the routing for early roads. *Courtesy the Imperial Calcasieu Museum.*

larger tribal cousins, living at the very frontier edge between the roaming plains tribes and the more village-oriented Native Americans of central and eastern Louisiana.

As a nomadic tribe driven by needs to hunt and gather seasonal foodstuffs, the Ishak did not leave large tangible villages or much in the way of solid artifacts. In fact, the relatively low numbers of Ishak were focused on self-preservation as small family- and clan-related tribal groups. Fierce fighters and agile hunters, the Ishak were never very numerous. Many succumbed to European-introduced disease and to near-constant skirmishes with the Chitimacha on the east and the Caddo and Natchez tribes on the north. Post-contact intermarriage with settlers also diluted the culture rapidly.

Today, there are a few descendants of the Ishak people in southwest Louisiana, and they are attempting to regain a tribal identity. Much of the challenge in establishing identity is that there are few physical remains or artifacts to attest to this near-lost culture. Rare items such as pottery, tools or arrowheads (made with traded-for chert or flint from northern and western sources) are in private and a few public collections. Many items are not particularly well documented. No villages or archaeological settlements remain. Occasionally, archaeologists find shell and artifact middens—essentially waste dumps—marking the location of seasonally reused settlement sites.

Some middens were harvested for the construction of shell roads in the 1920s and 1930s. A massive, alligator-shaped midden was photographed somewhere in Big Lake early in the twentieth century, with nothing remaining of that unique feature. According to some traditions, two of the ancient trails of the Ishak, one that connected the Sunrise people to their cousins in east Texas and the other connecting them to the trading Natchez and Caddo tribes to the north, eventually became the routings for the Old Spanish Trail to Texas and the Old Opelousas Road, respectively.

There was a strong oral tradition for ancestor Ishak, a cultural tradition that continues to characterize current tribal practice. Perhaps the best evidence of the oral tradition and of the ancient Ishak language is the word *Calcasieu* itself, which is the English transliteration of the Ishak word for "crying eagle." Crying Eagle was (and is) the honorific for the paramount chief of the Ishak tribe. This word was used by early Europeans to identify the river and the area. The Calcasieu River and Calcasieu Parish are two of the relatively few geographic entities in Louisiana with Native American names and perhaps the only ones named for a Native American person.

## THE FRENCH AND THE SPANISH MEET THE AMERICAN

Like most of Louisiana, Lake Charles was first viewed from the water. Early European explorers and settlers used the network of rivers and coastal waters to access and explore North America, skirting the coast and portaging over prairie to get to southwest Louisiana. Much of Louisiana history focuses on the heroic expeditions of LaSalle and others to claim the entire Mississippi valley and to explore and settle the central core of the continent.

However, the southwest corner of the state was not directly connected by water to the rest of Louisiana. For most of French colonial and Spanish colonial Louisiana history, Lake Charles was literally off the radar, viewed as a less than strategic part of the French settlement plan.

The French plan focused on water-connected "postes" like those in Natchitoches, Rapides (Alexandria), Opelousas and Attakapas and on trading the continent's riches through New Orleans to the mother country. Even when the French lost the core of the continent in the 1760s, the new Spanish authorities also viewed southwestern Louisiana in much the same light: it was remote, hard to get to and underpopulated—development could wait.

The American Revolution changed everything. The United States became a new player in the game for domination of the continent. In addition, the revolution ignited a continental change by helping to encourage uprisings in Europe. After the downfall of the French monarchy, Napoleon regained the central core of the continent back from the Spanish—Louisiana west of the Mississippi River—plus strategic New Orleans.

While less than a century old, the city of New Orleans was the prize of North American postcolonial strategy. It controlled access to the world for the goods of the entire center of the continent, including those of the newly won and settled American territories west of the Appalachians. Nearly as soon as Napoleon regained the Louisiana Territory, he offered it whole to the young American nation, a delegation from which had been in negotiations for access only to the city of New Orleans. The Louisiana Purchase instantly doubled the size of the United States and secured for the nation the valuable Mississippi valley, making modern America possible.

In the 1920s, the Old Spanish Trail followed the route of the Spanish across the coastal south to the Pacific. This view is of the Shell Beach Road section. *Courtesy McNeese University Archives.*

However, there was a problem. Napoleon, while generous with his offer of sale, was not particularly clear on some of the details. Specifically, the boundaries on the west were contestable if not actually in conflict with the geographic realities. The purchase included all the land drained by the Mississippi River to the west, a geographic definition based on the essential realities of drainage patterns. In the northern parts of the purchase territory (inhabited only by Native Americans), Lewis and Clark were soon to establish the drainage boundary limitations of the purchase. But south of the Red River—which clearly connected to the Mississippi—the lines and the intent of the sale were murky in territories that had been only lightly inhabited by creole colonists for three generations.

Much of southwest Louisiana was simply not part of the Louisiana Purchase. Plumbing-wise or otherwise, the land was clearly drained by streams that did not connect to the Mississippi. While waiting for the diplomats to draw the western boundary of America's new purchase, the commandants of the responsible federal and Spanish garrisons closest to the area in question made a simple gentleman's agreement about the disputed territory at their doorsteps.

In a practical sense, they agreed to leave the land alone and unclaimed. They agreed not to send in militia, customs officers or regulators of any sort. Any inhabitants there would be unprotected, ungoverned and untaxed. The commanding officer at the American fort in Natchitoches, Louisiana, and his counterpart in Nacogdoches, then capital of Spanish Texas, crafted the first "no man's land," or as it is sometimes called, "the neutral strip." They agreed not to recognize the other's claim, at least for the time being, until the diplomats drew their final lines, or until perhaps national objectives were clarified and re-focused.

At first, even deciding where the lines would be drawn for no man's land itself posed a problem. Some Americans believed that the Louisiana Purchase included all the land to the Rio Grande, a concept unacceptable to the sizable Spanish settlements in central and eastern Texas. The Spanish countered that the Tejas province reached to the Bayou Teche area, a mere seventy miles west of New Orleans.

In the end, practical matters set the boundaries of the new no man's land. The territories of settlers who regularly traded and moved goods to New Orleans were considered part of the purchase on the east, and the lands of those who traded and moved goods to San Antonio or Veracruz on the west were not. In between these two populations was No Man's Land, an irregular wedge from the Gulf northward to where Sabine Parish is located today. On a modern map, the western boundary would be between the Sabine and Neches Rivers and the eastern line somewhere east of the Calcasieu and definitely west of the Mermentau and the Red Rivers. Sparsely populated and holding no real strategic value, No Man's Land, the neutral strip, was of little immediate interest.

This wedge of No Man's Land was the status quo for nearly thirty years. During that time, Spain lost its Mexican colony, and the province of Texas began to agitate against Mexican rule. The strip served as sanctuary for a variety of settlers. Small numbers of "Texians," disenchanted Anglo settlers in the Spanish-ruled province, made their way east across the Sabine, and a few French-speaking Acadians drifted west from the Teche valley. During the War of 1812, the famous Battle of New Orleans made a hero of Andrew Jackson. Some of those who defended New Orleans made their way west after the war. Jean Lafitte, the other hero of the battle, visited and traded with the few scattered settlers in the Lake Charles area. When his days in New Orleans were over, he eventually established a second sanctuary by building an entirely new base at Galveston Bay, a site physically closer to southwest Louisiana.

While the Adams-Onis Treaty in 1819 set new boundaries and redrew maps, the era of No Man's Land would be ended only when the United States physically installed a military presence in this once-disputed territory. That military presence, a very modest but significant "Cantonment Atkinson," was opened on the eastern shore of Lake Charles. With that enterprise, the era of No Man's Land was over—at least for governing purposes. The United States had planted its flag on No Man's Land. However, socially and economically, the area would take longer to be fully assimilated into the still young nation and newly created state of Louisiana.

The establishment of that simple fort consolidated the western boundary of the state and of the United States. It marked the beginning of American control of the very southwest corner of the Louisiana Purchase and secured the international frontier with Mexico and, later, with the young Republic of Texas.

A marker stone on the shoreline of Lake Charles was installed by Sons and Daughters of the American Revolution. The marker tells the thumbnail story of Cantonment Atkinson and the end of No Man's Land. The cantonment itself was decommissioned in a few years, and the site was later sold to Thomas Bilbo and his wife, Ann Lawrence Bilbo, who set up their farm and mill on its grounds, actually living in the old barracks building for a time. The family made improvements on the property and eventually included a cemetery for family burials. Today, nothing remains of the barracks, the farm or the mill properties. But the ancient Bilbo Cemetery and the granite marker stone are still on the lakeside at the intersection of Interstate 10 and Lakeshore Drive, one of the gateway entrances to downtown Lake Charles. These mark the first real American claims to this corner of Louisiana.

## CREOLES, CAJUNS AND COWBOYS

Before 1763, the French promoted settlement with land grants in Louisiana using the same method they had perfected in the St. Lawrence valley in Canada. That French method was to slice river-edged land into long, thin parcels that had access to the river on one end and extended to the wilderness on the other. Lands along the Mississippi, the Teche, the Lafourche and the Red Rivers are defined by this ancient French practice of equally providing river access. While this practice, in theory, made sense in the very earliest days when water was the sole means of transportation, the amount of grantable land became limited—especially so when the plantation economy required larger and larger tracts to remain viable and when larger numbers of settlers began to migrate into the lower Mississippi valley.

As early as the 1770s, there is evidence of European colonial settlers in the area surrounding Lake Charles. But these few Spanish grants did not use the French colonial method for organizing real estate. The new Spanish administration provided land grants as individual, independent ranches, called *estacia*—or *vacheries* in the parlance of the time. Land grants were made to immigrants and to creoles (sons and daughters born in the New World of immigrants). The earliest land grants in the Lake Charles area are recorded as being made to Bartheleme LeBleu. These legitimate land grants were one form of settlement; land patents issued or reissued by some grantors was another; and some settlers simply operated without a formal issue of ownership.

The French Revolution, the slave uprising in Haiti and the expulsion and exile of Acadians from their homeland in Maritime Canada increased the stream of colonists and settlers to Louisiana and southwest Louisiana. Charles Sallier, the first European settler within the current city limits of Lake Charles, and Michel de Pithon, another early settler in the area that would become the city, were European refugees from the upheavals of the French Revolution and subsequent European wars.

A series of slave-led revolts in the Caribbean islands provided a second wave of immigration into Louisiana. Haitian refugees were sprinkled all over Spanish Louisiana and were readily assimilated into the then largely French-speaking majority.

The Acadian refugees were somewhat less easily assimilated. The Acadians, who had built a distinct culture in maritime Canada for 150 years, began to be exiled by the British in 1755. The British authorities continued to exile Acadians from their homeland in waves for another generation and a half. At first, the Spanish colonial authorities offered resettlement in the German Coast area north of New Orleans, but later resettlements had to include lands farther and farther from congested New Orleans and from the lucrative Mississippi valley. These settlement areas included the Teche, the Avoyelles and LaFourche areas and eventually the far western prairies of Louisiana.

The lands surrounding Lake Charles were exceptionally remote from the center of authority, regulation and control in New Orleans. This

Early twentieth-century cattle pens on the east end of Lake Charles would have been much the same a century earlier. Even the mascot of the local McNeese State University is the "cowboy." *Courtesy McNeese University Archives.*

isolation made far western Louisiana a sanctuary of sorts. And while the grassland prairies of southwestern Louisiana were viewed as unsuitable for the types of plantation agriculture—indigo, tobacco and, particularly, cotton and sugar cane—common in eastern and central Louisiana, it was suitable for small farms and ranches with open grazing, which was much the same culture the Acadians had created in Canada. The fact that most land remained essentially common allowed also for hunting, trapping and fishing, essential parts of the Acadian culture. Independent small holdings, subsistence farming and open grazing were also part of the Texian culture and that of many early settlers who practiced this type of agriculture in the southeastern states.

The creoles, the Acadians and other early settlers practiced and improved open-range cattle ranching. In sparsely populated regions distant from markets, cattle ranching was an obvious choice, relying as it does on relatively small numbers of workers—essentially cowboys on horseback—on lush, open grasslands. The trick to sustenance was getting the cattle to some sort of market, and the earliest pioneers did that by driving cattle eastward to markets in Opelousas, St. Martinville and even to New Orleans. Seasonal cattle drives eastward began in the Lake Charles area as early as the 1780s and continued until the era of rail. This was the birth of a true North American cowboy culture—caring for and driving cattle to market seasonally, one hundred years before the better-known cattle drives of Texas and Kansas.

The small crossroads settlement of Marion, just upriver from Lake Charles, was known as "the cattle town." It provided a secure place to ford livestock across the Calcasieu River and was used as such for at least four generations. The site of Marion was significant enough to have been selected as the first parish seat, and it was the location of the first parish courthouse. Today, Marion has been completely lost physically; it only provides part of the name of a consolidated high school in Lake Charles. Old Town Road follows the blaze-cut trail that led to Marion, now forever lost on the upper Calcasieu River.

## Pirates and Privateers

During colonial times and through the era of No Man's Land, the Gulf Coast, the Caribbean and the near Atlantic swarmed with pirates, privateers and buccaneers. True pirates were absolute outlaws, using gunfire and threats of death to capture and plunder legitimate vessels on the high seas. The vessels of the Spanish were particularly prized, as they carried the gold and silver of the New World. The range of true pirates was limitless: they were to be found on all oceans and seas, wherever treasure-laden vessels would shift from port to port. As particularly rich cargoes were run between Veracruz and Havana, and from those points in regular convoys to Seville and Cadiz in Spain, pirate lore focuses on the Gulf and Caribbean waters. Buccaneers were essentially pirates based in the Caribbean islands. The terms are similar in this context.

But privateers were entirely different, at least on paper. Privateers operated under "letters of marque" issued by legitimate countries. They flew national flags and were directed to board and plunder enemy ships (enemies of the countries issuing the letter of marque). The plunder was to be delivered to the nation of "marque" as spoils of war.

During the War of 1812, the United States itself provided letters of marque to privateers to board British ships and plunder British goods. Letters of marque were a recognized means of fighting wars and making reprisals. The U.S. Constitution describes the process in some detail.

It was not, however, the United States that provided letters of marque to the most famous of the privateers on the American Gulf Coast. Jean Lafitte and his brother Pierre flew the flag of Cartegena (in what would become Colombia in South America). Though they called themselves privateers—and maintained this distinction their entire lives—the world viewed the Lafittes as pirates, at least in how they delivered and profited from the goods they captured.

The Lafittes had operated a blacksmith shop in New Orleans for some time, but by 1805, the shop served merely as a front for their nefarious activities on the Gulf. Prior to that time, much of Jean Lafitte's life is conjectural. Much of his later career is also conjectural after his base in Galveston was abandoned in 1821 as part of an intense U.S. Navy sweep of illegal activities on the Gulf Coast. But between those dates, much is known about the "Gentleman Pirate."

The Lafittes were engaged in a very pragmatic mercantile enterprise for personal profit. They boarded any likely vessel, captured general cargoes at little to no cost and arranged for redistribution of that cargo through a network of agents throughout the upper Gulf Coast and the lower Mississippi River valley. The Lafitte enterprises captured and provided a wide range of consumer-ready goods—some gold and silver, of course, but also textiles, guns and gunpowder, various luxury goods including wines and spirits, even tools, furniture and household goods. These goods were supplied at much lower costs on a "black market" basis, without tariffs and without questions. The Lafittes simply eliminated the paperwork and the middlemen, simplifying the market process to their certain profit and skirting restrictive customs, tariffs and record-keeping by government bean-counters.

Goods seized by the Lafitte ships never saw the markets of Colombia. The Lafittes managed a respectable 25 percent (by some accounts) of all the trade in Louisiana, a fact that did not please William C.C. Claiborne, Louisiana territorial and later first state governor. The $500 bounty Claiborne offered for the head of Jean Lafitte was countered almost immediately by Lafitte's offer of a $1,500 bounty for the head of the governor. There was definitely a sense of humor in this contest of derring-do.

In Lake Charles, the various stories regarding Lafitte are related as family lore, told and retold from generation to generation. The tales include those of Lafitte's encounters with area pioneers Bartheleme LeBleu and his son Arsene (who admitted his long service as a Lafitte operative in many public documents in his later life). Lafitte certainly knew and transacted business with Lake Charles's pioneer and namesake, Charles Sallier, and with Michel de Pithon, both of whom were probably transported to this area on Lafitte ships if not by Lafitte himself.

The most colorful and romantic early Lake Charles tale is that of the amethyst brooch, which took place at Charles Sallier's winter cabin. While the cabin itself is long gone, it was physically located near the venerable Sallier Oak, a massive live oak tree estimated to be 375 or more years of age on the grounds of the Imperial Calcasieu Museum on Sallier Street.

This tale tells the story of an interrupted alliance between Lafitte and Charles Sallier's second wife, Catherine LeBleu Sallier. In this version, Charles, returning unexpectedly from a hunting trip, discovers Catherine in the arms of the charming pirate. In natural French jealous retaliation, Charles shoots at the couple. Catherine falls to the floor in a heap, Charles flees in instant remorse to die of a broken heart (in one version) after wandering the prairies alone. But Charles's errant bullet lodged not in Catherine's heart but in her new amethyst brooch—a token of affection that had just been bestowed on the beautiful young woman by the pirate himself. The bullet did not even scratch the skin—the jewelry literally saved Catherine's life. Whether the actual correspondent in this romantic tale was Lafitte himself (he would have been nearly sixty) or one of his operatives matters little. The local myth is about the romantic gentleman pirate Lafitte, who apparently hijacked hearts as well as shipboard cargoes. In reality,

Charles and Catherine lived on and reared six children to adulthood. Much later, the last daughter, Severine by name, formally dedicated a patch of the grounds nearby as Sallier Cemetery, to be used by the family and by their collaterals for burials.

Other great tales involve the alleged locations of buried pirate booty all over the general Lake Charles area. These legends are not based on any documented archaeological finds of hoards of gold or silver. Perhaps it is a truer statement that no treasure has ever been *reported* to have been found. Should privateer caches of coin or bullion ever be found in coastal Louisiana, it would likely be found in iron pots wrapped in waxed cloth or lead-lined casks. Treasure chests of wood were almost never used to store loot in the damp soils of the area.

While the various stories and versions of stories are romantic and perhaps a bit fanciful, documents do show that Lafitte maintained a major distribution point for trading goods at the mouth of what is now appropriately named Contraband Bayou, within the city limits of Lake Charles. The base, called a barracoon, was recorded as being in place between 1815 and 1822 with warehouses, staff quarters, a dock and a modest shipyard. It was part of perhaps a half dozen secure spots along the western half of the Gulf Coast provisioned first from Lafitte's Barataria base south of New Orleans and later by the pirate's Galveston-area base of Campeche. According to Lafitte operatives who remained in the Galveston area after Lafitte himself was exiled to the Caribbean, Lafitte had longstanding relationships with many early settlers in the Lake Charles area. Nothing of the barracoon exists today, as the site is part of the busy City Docks of the Port of Lake Charles.

# 2
# CRAFTING A CITY

## Crafting a City

Starting in the mid-1830s, the Bilbo farm along with neighboring pioneer Jacob Ryan's lakefront properties were subdivided into streets and development lots. The little community was commonly known as "the Lake" or sometimes "Charley's Lake" or "Charles Town," after Charles Sallier, who had been the earliest European settler in the general area.

Jacob Ryan is credited with being the "father of Lake Charles," but his extensive land patents ranged on both sides of the Calcasieu River. In addition, he was a force in shaping the entire early parish. He was a bit of a Renaissance man, operating a farm, a large cattle ranch and a forge as well as surveying, serving on various public committees and managing retail and wholesale businesses. He was elected to several offices and helped to bring in new settlers for this bit of civilization in southwest Louisiana.

Family lore says that, so driven was the man's phenomenal energy, when he personally surveyed the land to stake out the streets of the little community-to-be on his old farm, he did not notice that his surveyors' chain had caught in the root of a hackberry tree and thus was shortened. This kinked the layout for streets in downtown Lake Charles. To this day, there is a marked skew in the street grid orientation, with streets north of Division Street running perfectly north–south and east–west and those streets south of Division running slightly northeast to southwest. Interestingly, Division

This image of the swamp along Pithon Coulee—the south edge of downtown for one hundred years—contrasts strongly with today's cut-over swathe. *Courtesy the Imperial Calcasieu Museum.*

The channelized Pithon Coulee today is about as different from the historic view of the area as it can be. *From the author's collection.*

Street marked the boundary between the Bilbo farm on the north and the Ryan properties on the south, so there may be some truth to this city myth.

But the primary activity of Jacob Ryan, the enterprising "father of the city," was the cutting and processing of lumber. This was the primary building material of the mid-nineteenth century and a valuable resource. The waterways of southwest Louisiana were edged with millions of board feet of virgin cypress and the spectacular Calcasieu longleaf pine. While most of the lands to the east and south were prairie and marsh, terrain just north and west of Lake Charles held sizable reserves of these valuable trees, specimens two hundred and three hundred years old that provided long, straight and sturdy lumber, useful for building a city and valuable as a trading commodity. Ryan and most other early pioneers cut and shaped lumber, notching straight timbers for log cabins and crudely sawing boards in a whipsaw pit. Shingles were made by hand with a drawknife. Branches were used as firewood—no part was wasted. While much of the production was used to build their own homes, barns and commercial buildings, there was enough produced to use the surplus as a modest cash crop, shipped via river schooners to outside markets.

In the late 1840s and for another decade and a half, Germans and Frisian islanders migrated to Lake Charles expressly for the developing lumber industry, at which they excelled. They are credited with instituting a booming shipbuilding industry. Locally recruited by Captain Daniel Goos, the enterprising immigrants were part of the national influx of northern Europeans coming to the new United States, primarily to the Midwest but also to points in the South and West like Lake Charles. The original settlements of these Germans in Lake Charles are marked by German street names. Goosport was the original German settlement on the upper Calcasieu River. Streets named Fitzenreiter, Prater, Goos and Moeling, among others, outlined the once-independent community now entirely located within the city limits.

At first, lumber production was inefficient, with only man-powered pit saws and hand tools to shape timber. The introduction of steam-powered mills in the 1850s increased productivity and profits and increased the number of operating sawmills. The best example of the enterprise of early lumber pioneers is that of Captain Goos himself, who relocated a working sawmill from Mississippi. His three newly installed steam-powered upright sash saws were able to cut eleven thousand board feet daily, an unheard-of spike in productivity. Soon, his son-in-law George Locke operated his own new steam sawmill on Prien Lake. Together, they shipped out four million

This image of the Goos mill and shipyard shows the success of German industries on the upper Calcasieu. *Courtesy McNeese University Archives.*

board feet of cypress lumber to Galveston for sale during their first year of operation together.

In addition, the Goos family produced lumber for use by their shipyards, which crafted custom sailing schooners for the Gulf trade. And by 1857, the shipyard was able to launch a one-hundred-foot steamboat, modestly named the *Dan*. The *Dan* was expressly designed to tow, when needed, the four principal lumber-carrying trading schooners that had been built and were being operated by the Goos enterprises: the *Lehman*, the *Lake Charles*, the *Emma Thornton* and the *Winnebago*. The *Dan* would push or tow the vessels through and over the shallows of the lower Calcasieu River into the Gulf, where they would capture the winds to Galveston and to other ports. This lumber trading connection with Galveston continued for another sixty years. After the devastating 1900 storm that leveled most of that coastal metropolis, many structures were rebuilt using Calcasieu pine and cypress.

For almost four decades, hundreds of thousands of individual trees were branded, felled, limbed and dragged to the water to float to the mills lining the shore from Goosport to Prien Lake. Early reports of pre–Civil

Seen here is cut-over land and a far view of the steam-powered sawmills along the Calcasieu River and Lake Charles shorelines, taken in 1890. *Courtesy McNeese University Archives.*

War lumbering in Lake Charles record that visitors were able "to walk to West Lake" by stepping gingerly from one floating log to the next, so thickly covered was the lake that served as a holding pond for logs.

These early shipyards and sawmills along the river and lakefront are now gone, their waterfront locations literally erased by newer sawmills and, later, by continually improving railroad facilities, dredging and flood-control projects. Because of a relative scarcity of high, buildable land close to the river, there was a continuous competition to build bigger and better, erasing the old but essentially staying put on the same land.

Jacob Ryan's modest original sawmill—like all of the original antebellum sawmills of Goos, Locke, Bilbo and the few others—is long gone, now replaced by a string of commercial and trade buildings. The current Chase Bank Building at Broad Street and Lakeshore Drive in downtown Lake Charles marks the approximate site of that very first Ryan enterprise that set the city wheels in motion. The placid but now largely empty shores of the Calcasieu River north and east of the Salt Water Barrier mark the site of the once-bustling and now long-erased Goos enterprises.

## The Courthouse Caper

Only a few years after the Louisiana Purchase, the new state of Louisiana entered the Union with twenty-five civil subdivisions called parishes. (In the rest of the United States, these civil divisions are known as counties.) Remote southwest Louisiana was part of St. Landry Parish, which had been created by the earliest French colonial authority to administer the wild western frontier. To register land claims, to vote or to seek justice, one had to get to the venerable town of Opelousas, as much as two weeks' travel from southwest Louisiana by mule or carriage, one way.

By 1840, the population of this southwestern corner had grown to the point that a new parish needed to be created to ease the crisis. The western two-thirds of St. Landry was sheared off for the new parish of Calcasieu, named for the river that drained it. Even so, this new parish was still grand in scale, over 5,500 square miles (about the size of the state of Connecticut). But the travel times for necessary courthouse business would be reduced as much as 80 percent.

The old cattle-station crossroad, Marion, was selected as the parish town and the seat of the new courthouse. For twelve years, the Marion Courthouse served the scattered population of this state-sized parish. By 1851, after repeated failed efforts by Jacob Ryan (then sheriff) and by Samuel Kirby (the first trained lawyer in the parish) to relocate the parish courthouse to an even more central location (here, meaning more convenient to them), the two engineered a bold move. They would physically relocate the courthouse, records, jail and all to the new home they planned on the shoreline of "the Lake."

Two versions exist of how this grand enterprise was undertaken. One version involves an arduous overland haul of about twelve miles through woods, prairie and marsh using log rollers. The other involves a more leisurely ten-mile cruise on a barge. Whichever method Ryan and Kirby employed, the courthouse was relocated to a patch of lakeshore ground given by the generous Samuel Kirby. A letter was dispatched to the crenellated state capitol in Baton Rouge that the parish seat of Calcasieu had been relocated to "Charley's Lake."

The transplanted 1840 courthouse was replaced with an updated wooden building by 1853; a grander Empire-styled courthouse followed in 1891. The turn-of-the-century boom in the parish and the city required a considerable 1902 addition on the east side of the 1891 courthouse. This doubled the size of the building and provided a neoclassical decorative façade along with a modest tower.

This is a rare view of the 1891 courthouse. A 1902 addition to the front of this building doubled its size, creating a long, thin courthouse. It was lost in the Great Fire of 1910. *Courtesy McNeese University Archives.*

That doubled-length courthouse was the one that burned to the ground in the Great Fire of 1910. It was replaced with the current grand Historic Calcasieu Courthouse of 1911, designed by trophy architects of the day, Favrot and Livaudais. On the grounds of the current courthouse are two modest stacked white stones, the cornerstones of the 1891 version and of its 1902 addition. Interestingly enough, the site of the contemporary building housing the day-to-day workings of the court, the Calcasieu Judicial Center at the corner of Kirby Street and Lakeshore Drive, is almost exactly where the 1840 courthouse was sited after its relocation from Marion.

## Civil War and Cemeteries

In 1857, with the transplanted courthouse rooted to the shore of the lake, the population of Charley's Lake, by then also called Charles Town and simply "the Lake," determined that a more dignified name was needed for the young town. The name "Charleston" was selected (in honor of the first European settler) and the town incorporated. It is probable that the focus on Charleston, South Carolina, just before the outbreak of the Civil War in 1861 encouraged the little settlement to select the name over the other possibilities as a show of support for the South.

Besides setting up a police force, a set of aldermen and a mayor, one of the necessary actions of the Corporation of Charleston was to establish a public burying ground for Protestants. There were several family cemeteries already in place, such as the Bilbo Cemetery, the Sallier burial grounds and the Goos Family Graveyard, to tend to the needs of those families and their collaterals. There was also a cemetery for Catholics donated by William Hutchins in 1861. But there was nothing in place for Protestants. To remedy this omission, viewed as a serious impediment to growth and public order, the corporation purchased the half city block bounded by Belden, Moss and Church Streets for Corporation Cemetery, listed on some plats as Magnolia Cemetery.

Unfortunately, there was no great outcry in the 1950s and 1960s when the center of the block with Corporation Cemetery was being cleared out for what would become Interstate 10. The unique geography of the area literally forced the routing of that highway through the core of a long-established neighborhood. With some due warning, many families relocated ancestral remains from Corporation Cemetery to other cemeteries. However, not all remains were claimed, and some records were lost. (Burials had been discontinued at Corporation some sixty years earlier.) A thin slice of the cemetery remains, still in the dutiful care of the city. What remains of Corporation Cemetery can be seen at the northeast corner of Moss and Church Streets.

Mount Hope was typical of the sawmills that developed in the middle of the nineteenth century in Lake Charles. *Courtesy the Imperial Calcasieu Museum.*

The early Civil War was relatively quiet in the Lake Charles area; in 1862, a small squad of Union troops under the command of Lieutenant Fred Crocker made a successful raid on the lake and burned three ships being used as blockade runners. They also captured the *Dan*, the steamboat tug that had towed the blockade runners over the shallows of the Calcasieu. But the area was mostly quiet for the rest of the war. Lake Charles men served in battles throughout the war. But the closest skirmishes and battles were away at Calcasieu Pass at the mouth of the river, at Niblett's Bluff to the west and at Sabine Pass to the far southwest. The major campaigns of the Red River and Teche were far to the north and east of Lake Charles.

There was a reported surprise encounter of scouting parties from both the Union and Confederate sides on the river near Lake Charles that ended with a conciliatory barbecue hosted by the Goos family at their home. This may be anecdotal. While there were partisans and strong sentiments for both the North and South in the area, Lake Charles and most of southwest Louisiana were simply not part of the antebellum plantation society and economy that characterized so much of Louisiana. There were no major plantations of sugar or cotton and no targets of war to gain or to protect. Much of the war was waged around, but not directly in, Lake Charles.

The aftermath of the war was more significant. The investment of new capital and the introduction of new settlers on an unprecedented scale meant big changes in the young town. In Lake Charles, these new settlers, particularly the ones bringing in new capital and making big changes, are known as "the Michigan Men" rather than the more derisive term *carpetbaggers* used in other parts of the South. The Michigan Men would help convert a once-isolated cow town into a relatively prosperous community.

# 3
# INGREDIENTS FOR GROWTH

## THE MICHIGAN MEN

The decades that followed the end of the Civil War brought significant changes to southwest Louisiana and to the young town. The first change involved renaming the young town and its incorporation as a city. Perhaps as an act of atonement, or perhaps just to turn over a new leaf, the little community rid itself of the Charleston moniker and incorporated itself formally as Lake Charles in 1867.

Reconstruction in the South meant the introduction not only of new rules and regulations but also of new settlers and new investment capital—much of it Northern—to fully exploit what resources were available in what amounted to occupied territory. Parts of the state of Louisiana had been occupied early in the war, and the state as a whole would remain under martial law until 1877. While the excesses of carpetbagger and scalawag politics and economics ranged wide, from Shreveport to New Orleans and beyond, southwest Louisiana and Lake Charles were not particularly affected in a negative sense. The plantation economy in place in the rest of the state made Louisiana a cherished target of Union troops, but as this was not the economy of southwest Louisiana to any great degree, the options for gross political mismanagement were limited.

The return to peace meant a return to business. In the 1870s, the H.C. Drew Lumber Company's steam mill was operational, and others soon

Michigan Men built grand houses that featured rare figured cypress and exotic hardwoods in the interior. The Nason House is seen in this period image. *Courtesy McNeese University Archives.*

followed, including Bradley-Ramsay, Mount Hope, J.A. Bel, Drew and Powell, Lake City Mills, J.C. Stout, Hodges Fence and Lumber and the Calcasieu Lumber Company. At the end of the century, the city's processing capacity was nearly a half-million board feet per day.

While not the first Michigan Man in Lake Charles, William Ramsay was one of the most industrious. He developed an interest in Calcasieu cypress as early as 1879. His story is instructive and typical. Born in Canada, Ramsay entered the business in Michigan to concentrate on the pine of that state. Hearing highly favorable reports from scouts in southwest Louisiana, he organized the Bradley-Ramsay Lumber Company and financed the largest sawmill constructed up to that time in Lake Charles. He eventually controlled 150,000 acres of virgin woods to the north and west of the city.

He famously sent samples of the distinctive cypress and, later, heart pine, to hundreds of northern contractors and brokers. He promoted the woods as superior for all forms of industrial construction and building of bridges, ships and rails. He also lauded the material as unmatched for high-end millwork. His efforts paid off, as he was soon exporting lumber by rail to points north, east and west and by schooner and steamer to the port of Galveston, to New Orleans and to ports on the Atlantic and Caribbean coasts. He expanded his operations to include the purchase of a rival mill and added specialty mill shops that fabricated windows, doors, shingles and shutters. To streamline operations he built drying kilns, warehouses and a short-line railroad to open up additional timberlands. In time, he had more than 15 million board feet of lumber as disposable inventory. The Ramsay mills were the largest employer with the largest payroll in the city for two decades. Plus, the Ramsay mills paid regular wages in currency rather than using the common practice of paying employees in script only useable at company commissaries and mercantile stores. Paying regular wages in cash put money into circulation and encouraged other enterprises.

Ramsay was a partner in many Lake Charles businesses, including the Majestic Hotel and at least two construction contracting companies that used his own products. He personally financed a variety of mercantile and business ventures on the side. In 1906, he sold out to the Long-Bel Lumber Company and retired to California, where he died in 1909. The Long-Bel Companies, based in Kansas City, continued and improved operations. However, as the virgin timber disappeared under the saw, the firm moved operations northward and westward, eventually abandoning Lake Charles entirely in the 1920s.

The Ramsay Mansion, still standing on the corner of Broad and Ford Streets, was constructed as his personal home in Lake Charles. Like many Michigan Man houses, the mansion showcased the various products that were available at his mill. Perhaps as many as fifteen still-standing grand houses on Broad Street and in the surrounding residential area can be characterized in this way. Another fifteen to twenty grand Michigan Man homes have been lost to neglect, arson, demolition or redevelopment and are remembered only in old photographs and postcards. But while these singular grand houses and many other more modest Victorian-era and early twentieth-century homes in Lake Charles testify to the wealth and productivity of those sawmills, no physical evidence remains of the industry itself in the city. While still beautifully forested in some locations of the city, the virgin cypress and pine are also gone and lost forever.

Every industrial facility that cut and shaped wood; made window sashes, shutters and doors; planed siding; or fabricated shingles was relocated to greener fields as the lumber played out in southwest Louisiana. If the mill itself failed to follow the trees, it was simply abandoned as obsolete, sold

The Ramsay Mansion began as the home of the Michigan Man William Ramsay. It was later a bed-and-breakfast and today serves as a site for professional offices. *From the author's collection.*

The Chester Brown House balcony does not connect to the columns but hangs from the porch ceiling. The columns, slightly tapered, paneled and square, are identified as "the Lake Charles column" for their use in many houses throughout the area. *From the author's collection.*

for redevelopment or allowed to deteriorate in the weather. Some sawmill equipment starting life in Lake Charles ended productive careers as far away as the Pacific Northwest, having made stops in north Louisiana, Arkansas, Texas or even Oregon.

At the height of the lumber industry in Lake Charles, as many as seventeen facilities processed millions of board feet of dimensional lumber and railroad ties, with creosote mills, shingle mills, mills for doors and sash, warehouse and kilns being the primary types.

Occasionally, an abandoned railroad spur or a lumber camp cut is discovered even within the city. From time to time, divers retrieve sinker cypress logs from the bottom of the Calcasieu River or from one of the lakes, elements from the heyday of lumber. Most evidence of the timber cut and transformed by the mills of Lake Charles is lost to time. It's an entire industry erased.

Still, the products of that industry are still seen in the variety of residential properties constructed between 1860 and 1930 in the Charpentier Historic

District, in the Margaret Place Historic District and in older parts of the city. The majority of those houses were constructed with lumber actually processed in the city of Lake Charles. It's the tangible evidence of the once-potent industrial giant, evidence that needs protection if it is to tell an important chapter of city history.

## Railroads Rule

The end of the Civil War in 1865 meant that the railroads could again begin the process of connecting communities in earnest. While short-line rail had been in place in Louisiana prior to the Civil War, in the decades following the war, these lines were extended, expanded and merged, connecting hitherto isolated communities and markets. The Morgan and Louisiana Railroad, later the Texas and New Orleans and, eventually, the Southern Pacific, continued westward across the Louisiana marsh and prairie, expanding and changing names and lives in the process. Eventually, the line connected New Orleans to Houston and points west—providing a safe and reliable connection to Lake Charles.

The changes wrought by the reliable and quick rail connections were immense. Until the opening of the first rail depot, travel to Lake Charles had been haphazard and difficult, involving a time-consuming combination of water and overland travel. A trip to Lake Charles from New Orleans prior to the 1870s involved a three-day steamboat trek down the Mississippi to the Gulf and up the Atchafalaya to the Teche, disembarking at the ancient port town of Washington near Opelousas. From there, travelers faced a three- to five-day ride by mule or carriage. By water alone, a traveler had no scheduled passenger service from New Orleans at all, and travelers to the young town had to rely on irregular cargo-carriers, which could take weeks. With the opening of Lake Charles's Louisiana-Western Depot in 1878, travel time was reduced to eight hours, with allowances for the train ferries in Brashear City and at New Orleans.

The transcontinental Southern Pacific line not only connected communities strung along its route, but it also operated a series of short-line rail to communities not on the main line. In Lake Charles, the freshly constructed Southern Pacific depot (1899)—which replaced the earlier Louisiana Western depot (1878 to 1899) located nearby—handled not only trains going east and west for nearly a century but also trains headed north on a short-lived Lake Charles and Northern spur that ran via

Moss Bluff and Gillis. Located at the heart of Railroad Avenue near Bilbo Street, the 1899 Southern Pacific Passenger depot was lost to fire in 1984, and its matching freight depot was demolished for safety reasons shortly thereafter.

Two other rail lines played roles in the shaping of the young town. Both lines linked Lake Charles with points north and northeast, and both lines were the products of strongly driven entrepreneurs for whom rail was the means to expand markets and to make profits.

Rail connections to Alexandria, Louisiana, and points north and east were made possible by the Watkins rail line, later called the Iron Mountain. It was eventually enveloped by Missouri-Pacific Railroad. The Watkins line was created by the intensive investment of Jabez Bunting Watkins of Lawrence, Kansas, to serve as a means of supporting and promoting his revolutionary real estate plans for southwest Louisiana.

None of the historic railroad depots remains, although the Amtrak passenger stop uses some of the cast-iron brackets from the old Southern Pacific station. Here is the site marker for the Iron Mountain–Missouri Pacific depot. *From the author's collection.*

Watkins, a pioneering real estate master developer, conceived of and sold the idea of fresh starts in a frost-free paradise of multiple harvests to thousands of midwesterners seeking new opportunities. To access these acres and to provide reliable transportation, he financed and constructed a rail line originally planned to end at the Gulf itself. However, due to the unique geography of the coastal marsh, it ended its southward trek in Lake Charles. The Watkins/Iron Mountain/Missouri Pacific depot, circa 1892—actually the terminus, since the line went no farther—was on the southeast corner of Ryan and Clarence Streets in Lake Charles. The terminal was abandoned and demolished in the late 1960s. Watkins freight was handled by multiple spur rail lines built throughout central Lake Charles and in the surrounding countryside and intensively used until improved highways and truck service displaced rail as the primary mover of local freight beginning in the 1940s. Most of the spur lines in central Lake Charles were abandoned in the 1950s and '60s, and some were later removed for redevelopment of railroad-owned property.

Pictured is the Ann Street side of the Kelly-Weber wholesale warehouse on spur lines of the Kansas City Southern railroad, whose depot was on the same block. *Courtesy the Imperial Calcasieu Museum.*

Another entrepreneur, this time with the grand notion of connecting Kansas City and the Midwest to the Gulf, was Arthur Stilwell, whose Kansas City Southern main line began to edge southward in 1887, eventually connecting Shreveport with DeQuincy, Louisiana, and on to Port Arthur, Texas. A spur line connected Lake Charles with this line. The Lake Charles spur ended first at a short-lived Union Station (circa 1894) at Front Street and Lawrence Street (now Pryce Street), a site that later served as a railroad repair yard. In 1925, a mission-style Kansas City Southern depot was constructed at Ryan and Lawrence Streets. It served rail passengers and freight traffic until the 1950s and was abandoned and demolished as obsolete in 1989.

In addition to the main railroad stations that provided scheduled passenger service, each of the competing rail lines operated a series of short-line spurs that followed local agricultural and industrial needs. These spurs crisscrossed the region to serve the developing cattle, rice, sulfur, lumber and petrochemical industries. In addition to providing short- and long-haul transportation of people and goods, the railroads operated lucrative land leases adjoining their railroad rights-of-way. In the heyday of rail, the three competing depots in Lake Charles had as many as twenty-five arrivals and departures daily to points east, north and west. In addition, the railroads controlled a significant percentage of real estate to include distribution warehouses, factories and other businesses on leased railroad land.

## WATER CONNECTIONS

The interconnected transportation offerings of short-line spurs and long-line scheduled rail services were enhanced by two principal working steam ferryboats in operation in the late nineteenth and early twentieth centuries. These vessels connected Lake Charles with the western shore and with communities downriver.

Prior to the era of steam transportation, trade on the water was conducted by privately owned and operated sailing schooners, generally shallow-draft vessels, most less than seventy-five feet in length. These vessels were long proven on Gulf coastal waters, both freshwater and saltwater, nimble enough to proceed under sail even with scant winds and small enough to be poled or paddled if necessary in shallows. A few early steam-powered tugs, like the *Dan*, helped with shallows and shoals, but German-immigrant-built schooners served Lake Charles from the earliest days of settlement until the 1920s. But the era of steam provided more regular and dependable service. The two most famous ferryboats serving Lake Charles were the *Borealis Rex* and the *Hazel*.

The *Borealis Rex* had its berth at the foot of Pujo Street at the water. The *Rex*, built in 1888 for use on the upper Mississippi River, was bought secondhand for use on the Calcasieu. The *Rex* was the popular deluxe overnight round-trip ferry between Cameron and Lake Charles. Beginning in 1905, it carried passengers and freight—everyone from preachers to salesmen and everything from groceries to cattle—on its three runs per week. The *Rex* was much more regular, more comfortable and more accommodating than any of the schooners that had sailed that route. Its career ended abruptly in 1930, when the U.S. Mail contract was won by a speedier gas-powered vessel. Ironically, that year also marked the opening of the first graveled road to Cameron, making vehicular traffic possible and marking the end of public-scheduled ferry service in Lake Charles.

The secondhand *Borealis Rex* steamboat provided first-class ferry service during an important period of area growth. *Courtesy McNeese University Archives.*

Looking east toward the distant downtown on the far side, you can trace the lower Calcasieu River flowing toward the City Docks through the 1916 bridge. *Courtesy the Imperial Calcasieu Museum.*

The *Borealis Rex* was literally abandoned at the now-disused ferry landing. Metal from its deteriorating superstructure and engine was eventually donated to World War II scrap drives. The great steering wheel was salvaged and is on display at the Imperial Calcasieu Museum, one of the few remnants of the *Rex* on view. The design of the steering wheel was incorporated into the logos and seals for both the City of Lake Charles and the Port of Lake Charles, with detail modifications to distinguish one from the other.

The smaller and older ferry steamer *Hazel* transported passengers and freight to Westlake and to Bagdad and onward to Texas several times daily. The *Hazel* was the last cross-river ferry in a line of service ferries beginning just after the Civil War. Ferry service started with rope ferries as early as 1840 that connected east and west Calcasieu, and many early roadways memorialized famous ferry landings in their names, such as Anthony Ferry, Dunn Ferry, Perkins Ferry, Goos Ferry and others.

The *Hazel* was discontinued and sold off after the 1916 Old Spanish Trail Bridge was completed at the foot of Shell Beach Road. The new bridge connected Lake Charles with the routing of the federally sponsored Old Spanish Trail (later U.S. Highway 90) to Westlake and onward to Texas. The road improvements made the *Hazel* ferry service obsolete. In less than four decades, the Old Spanish Trail Bridge itself would be declared obsolete and demolished (except for the western approaches) when the "new" four-lane "Pistol Bridge" was opened on the new routing of Highway 90 through Lake Charles. The western approaches of the Old Spanish Trail Bridge can still be seen from the western foot of Shell Beach Drive at the river.

The area still has a rich marine and maritime culture, with several active shipyards catering to fishing, oil production and pleasure craft, as well as a flotilla of various diesel and internal combustion vessels. But the great age of working watercraft shifting passengers and light freight has largely gone by the wayside.

# The Streetcar

The urban link in the transportation network connecting Lake Charles to the wider world was the streetcar. One of only five Louisiana cities to ever have such an upscale civic amenity, Lake Charles's version began in 1891 with mule-driven cars on a single line connecting Railroad Avenue with Ryan Street. By 1905, all lines were fully electrified and expanded citywide. At the system's height, five full routes reached from Cessford

A 1907 view downtown at Ryan and Kirby Streets shows the streetcar. In the background is the Calcasieu State Bank. The building with pointed arches in the right foreground is part of the Catholic church, convent and school. *Courtesy McNeese University Archives.*

Street in the north to Gulf Street in the south and from Lake Street to First Avenue, essentially providing streetcar service to most residents of the young city.

In addition to the Gulf States Utility electric streetcar system, the Watkins railroad operated the "Dummy-line" streetcar from 1893 until 1906. Via Broad Street and First Avenue, the Dummy-line Streetcar connected freight operations, businesses and warehouses in the Avenues area east of Enterprise Boulevard and the railcar shops in Goosport to downtown Lake Charles. For a short time, these two streetcar systems provided a means for students to get to the new Lake Charles High School—then considered to be on the far eastern side of the city on Boulevard. While the Dummy-line ceased operations in the first decade of the twentieth century, the principal Lake Charles electric streetcar system continued almost until the 1930s.

All the streetcars were running at the time of the Great Fire of 1910 and famously provided transportation for residents fleeing the fire and for firefighters rushing to battle the inferno. After the fire, in an effort to grow the city outward, streetcar services expanded yet again and improved lines in all directions.

In the increasingly busy city, the streetcars provided consistent and regular service. For a time, streetcars ran twenty-four hours a day and seven days a week, a remarkable public transportation concept even today. The lines connected homes with workplaces, schools, churches, theaters and places of amusement. Ryan Street famously had two lines that served the core of the city from Railroad Avenue in the north to where the lines split at South Street (now the extension of Ryan Street and the street now called Dr. Michael DeBakey Drive). One line tracked west along South Ryan and the other eastward to Hodges Street along what was then called Miller Avenue (now Seventh Street).

While the main spine of the streetcar system ran along Ryan Street from Railroad Avenue (known in those rough-and-ready days as "Battle Row") to the foot of South Ryan Street at Lake Street, suburban extensions continued on Kirby Street eastward to Kirkman, to Lawrence (now Pryce), then north

The five-line streetcar system relied on loyal teams, particularly when the system operated seven days a week and twenty-four hours a day. *Courtesy McNeese University Archives*.

via Boulevard and Opelousas Street to Cessford Street in Goosport. The Cessford line had wound its way into the community of Goosport, serving its shipyards, lumber mills, warehouses and working neighborhoods. Another line proceeded eastward down Miller (Seventh Street) along Hodges Street to Tenth Street and south on Kirkman toward the brickyards, the fairgrounds and a racetrack located off Gulf Street (near the location of T.S. Cooley Magnet School today).

The original streetcar subdivision, Margaret Place, was well positioned to access the downtown business district, the working factory and mills district on the water and the recreational facilities on the southwest end of town. The South Ryan Line connected to the entire city and ended at the popular Shell Beach at Walnut Grove and Barbe Pleasure Pier and Casino, all of which were literally at the end of the line. Margaret Place had been developed on the Margaret Perkins farmstead south of the Pithon Coulee swamp just after the Great Fire. Other streetcar-served subdivisions included "Central Place" in the neighborhoods near Good Shepherd Church and the upper Hodges Street/West Common Street neighborhood. The entire city benefited from improved streetcar access to education, jobs, church and entertainment.

Streetcars were an impetus to developing a more sophisticated and prosperous Lake Charles. Without ownership of a horse and carriage, personal transportation was limited to the distance one was able to walk. With streetcars, the city was an open book for its residents and visitors.

The old Perkins farmhouse stood on what would become Margaret Place after the great fire. *Courtesy McNeese University Archives.*

The Pleasure Pier, built in 1907, was a popular venue for dances, concerts and other recreations. *Courtesy McNeese University Archives.*

The streetcars connected homes with workplaces, businesses, libraries, shops, railroad depots, ferry landings, churches and even amusement centers. Promotional tie-ins encouraged ridership to entertainment sites such as fairgrounds, racetracks and pleasure piers. The pleasure piers were particular favorites, constructed over the cooling waters of the lake and famous for dances, theatrical exhibitions and socials. The early fairgrounds and a racetrack were located at the end of the Hodges streetcar extension. Promotions, cultural attractions, sports events and entertainments regularly scheduled at the piers, the racetracks and the fairgrounds made use of the streetcars for public advertisement, and the streetcars benefited from the increased number of fares.

But by 1925, the entire streetcar system in Lake Charles, like streetcar systems nationwide, was facing stiff competition from private motor cars, independent buses and truck traffic. After the untimely death of J.A. Landry, the streetcar utility's greatest civic booster and stockholder, the system changed ownership several times, reduced services and folded in 1927. At that time, most of the routes were served by a new bus service. While most of the streetcar rolling stock was sold off, the last streetcar in Lake Charles served as the home of a diner-styled café located near Iris and Bilbo Streets. The old diner, abandoned, was demolished in 1939.

Occasionally, streetcar tracks are unearthed when repairs or new construction is undertaken in downtown Lake Charles. A short length of the Ryan Street double tracks was unearthed when post–Hurricane Rita improvements were made at the Pithon Coulee Bridge and at the Clarence Street intersection. However, there is little physical evidence of the four decades when Lake Charles was served by streetcars.

## J.B. Watkins and the Selling of Southwest Louisiana

Perhaps the greatest population growth of the city in the second half of the nineteenth century was due to the marketing efforts of real estate mogul Jabez Bunting Watkins. Beginning in 1880, Watkins's remarkable interest in coastal Louisiana's promise created a company that bought 1.5 million acres of land in southwest Louisiana. He found capital to finance a railroad to that land and dug canals with steam-powered pumps to drain low areas and upgrade the real estate. His company resold lots, farms, homesteads and entire townships. At the same time, other Watkins enterprises were harvesting lumber, managing crops and grazing and, eventually, profiting from oil and gas production on yet-unsold lands.

Watkins made early use of direct mail, self-financing purchases on credit and bundling package deals for qualified buyers. This modern-sounding and still-revolutionary enterprise was made possible by an intricate working model that included newspaper and direct-mail advertising agencies; loans and collections through Watkins's own national bank; and promotion and use of his own railroads, construction companies, suppliers and liveries. Watkins company brochures assured chilly midwesterners that multiple harvests were possible in frost-free coastal Louisiana and that his reliable rail system would be able to transport their oranges to market on the very same day they were harvested. It was a marketer's dream come true. Later in life, Watkins sold his interest in the North American Land and Timber and related companies and retired to Kansas, where he began his real estate career.

While the Watkins enterprises were generally rurally focused, the central point of service, the urban core that provided the necessary retail, wholesale, education, transportation, banking and opportunity connections was Lake Charles. It was also the center for independent entrepreneurism, with some of the transplanted midwesterners choosing to pursue careers in relatively urban Lake Charles rather than on the lonely prairies of Sweetlake, Vinton and Thornwell.

To promote sales of land, the Watkins organizations had to drain low areas to reclaim them for agricultural purposes just east of Lake Charles in the late nineteenth century. *Courtesy McNeese University Archives.*

The Watkins Bank at Broad and Hodges Streets was part of the promotion, marketing and financial wheels of the enterprise that changed the lives of thousands of new settlers. *Courtesy the Imperial Calcasieu Museum.*

Particularly notable are the stories of the origin of the Kelly-Weber family of companies that began their very successful businesses with the Palace Grocery Store on Ryan Street, as well as the Rock family of Kansas, who relocated southward and eventually owned several hardware and dry goods stores in the region. Many midwesterners invested or worked in the lucrative lumber business and made connections with Michigan Men investors. The principal operating branch of the Watkins National Bank was located on Broad Street at Hodges, and the principal station for the Watkins railroad was on Ryan at Clarence. J.B. Watkins, for all practical purposes, was a king in his domain of finance, real estate and transportation.

Watkins made every effort to fulfill the rural agricultural paradise he promoted and promised. He touted transportation improvements, like new graveled roads, and encouraged educational improvements to the young communities he was creating in the midst of his vast landholdings. Watkins donated land and funds for public schools. He encouraged the purchase of the Acadia College site for a new expanded high school, viewed at the time as an extravagance. The site had been a grand but failed experiment of the Congregational church on the rough eastern side of town. Watkins made the purchase possible and allowed the use of his Dummy-line streetcar to ferry students to the three-story structure, the start of Lake Charles High School.

Watkins also engaged the considerable talents of pioneer agronomist Seamon K. Knapp, bringing the dean of scientific American agriculture to southwest Louisiana to assist in transforming the prairies and marsh to arable cropland. Knapp, once head of the progressive agriculture school in the state of Iowa, established model demonstration farms in southwest Louisiana; introduced steam-powered cultivators, harvesters and pumps; and instituted advanced farm-to-market practices, pest-control procedures and agricultural hygiene.

These efforts jump-started large-scale agriculture in the area. Within two decades, the saw-grass prairies that had been marginal rangeland for generations began to produce bumper crops of rice and large profits for farmers. Such was the astronomical rise of the importance of rice that, by 1912, the hundred-weight price of American rice was set on the docks of the Lake Charles mills. By 1926, the largest rice mill in the world had been erected in the city of Lake Charles to service the expanding range of rice.

Rapid growth of the rice industry encouraged the building of the world's largest rice mill in Lake Charles. *Courtesy McNeese University Archives.*

Swift Meat Packing Plant was constructed just east of Lake Charles in the 1930s. Only the name "Swift Plant Road" remains of the once impressive facility. *Courtesy McNeese University Archives.*

Inevitable market changes, expansions of arable land for rice and advances in processing eventually moved the epicenter of rice cultivation to other locations. Modern evidence of rice as king of the city is scant; the largest rice mill and many of its local competitors became obsolete and slowly reduced output, selling off parts and equipment and eventually succumbing to fire and general deterioration. By 1980, the once-largest rice mill in the world was gone, its site on the Calcasieu River overgrown with grass. However reduced from its former position as king, the production and transportation of rice is still a major factor in Lake Charles's economy.

Knapp made improvements in animal husbandry and hygiene that enhanced and expanded the cattle market. Investments included several late nineteenth-century meatpacking plants in the Lake Charles area that processed hundreds of head of cattle per week for local consumption and for trade. Production improvements, refrigeration and the expansion of the market made possible a six-story, state-of-the-art Swift meatpacking plant in the early part of the twentieth century constructed just outside Lake Charles city limits. As to the dairy industry, at its height, three processing milk-and-cream plants handled regional needs. The last local dairy, Guth, shut operations in the 1980s as the dairy market in America shifted to efficient long-distance production rather than regional production. Now lost, the Swift Plant is remembered only by the name of the road on which it was located. And while both the Borden's and Walker-Roemer dairies are long gone, the physical plant of the shuttered Guth Dairy still remains on Hodges Street just south of downtown.

Watkins made sure that transportation, marketing and scientific agricultural advances made for productive harvests and for contented new settlers in the countryside. That same mix of macro-planning and attention to detail spurred growth in Lake Charles. The investments made by Michigan Men, along with the promotions and interconnected planning of J.B. Watkins, were effective, productive and profitable. A rare combination of idea, opportunity and resources grew both population and possibilities for a young Lake Charles.

## Enterprise

In the three decades following the introduction of rail, the population of Lake Charles grew fourfold, including immigrants from foreign lands and settlers from other parts of the United States. A significant percentage of the midwesterners who were encouraged to relocate to southwest Louisiana were second-generation German, British and Irish settlers. Their parents or grandparents had emigrated from the old country and first settled in the American Midwest. In addition to the relocation of these midwesterners, there were also large numbers of immigrants from Syria and Lebanon; newcomers from Italy, Denmark, Hungary and Scandinavia; and Jews from France and Germany.

Perhaps the most enterprising story of the immigrant spirit is that of Julie Muller, who started Lake Charles's most complete department store in 1882. Julie was born in Alsace, then a part of France, in 1854. After the Franco-Prussian War, she immigrated to New Orleans and there married Isadore Muller. They had a son, Maurice, and a daughter, Dora. When Isadore died in a yellow fever epidemic, the now-widowed Julie, who had worked as a successful dressmaker in New Orleans, decided to relocate to Lake Charles in 1882 with her children. She opened a shop on Ryan Street and lived over the shop. The enterprise proved successful, and she later constructed a two-story building. Her business expanded with the rapid growth of the area. She married Simon Marx in 1891.

By 1913, her son Maurice Muller, who inherited the business, built a modern three-story building, then the largest in southwest Louisiana, with the first commercial elevator. He expanded the lines the store carried; for a time, Muller's sold everything from corsets to caskets, clothing to dry goods, as well as shoes, rugs, jewelry, curtains and furniture. Adolf Marx, Maurice's half brother, took command in 1930 and added air-conditioning to the building and then expanded the structure in 1943 and again in 1950, which doubled its size. He also added the famous "moving stairs," the first regional application of escalators. Muller's opened two branches in the 1970s, one in the new, enclosed Prien Lake Mall in south Lake Charles and another in DeRidder, Louisiana.

Finally, in 1985—103 years after its founding—Muller's closed, victim of the general economic downturn at a time when it was unable to compete with expanding national retailers. Subsequently, the building was donated to parish government. The structure was later purchased and renovated into residential lofts with ground-floor retail. It is part of the revival and reuse of downtown Lake Charles. The Muller's building is individually listed in the National Register of Historic Places, but the real testament of the power of this department store is that, to this day, former employees still regularly meet and reminisce about the decades when Muller's was the place to shop in southwest Louisiana. Muller's retail history is significant for its staying power and close connections to the community it served.

Ryan Street, the crossroads of the community, was also the center for much of the other retail and business activities by new immigrants and settlers. The King and the Weber families, midwestern in origin, formed the Kelly-Weber group, which began with retail on Ryan Street and later grew to a widely diversified business enterprise with wholesale, real estate, insurance, timber and shipping interests added to its retail origins. The Gordon and Von Phul Drugstore, also a product of midwestern relocation, grew to a network of multiple locations in the city under the Gordon's Drugs nameplate. The original building still stands at the corner of Ryan and Pujo.

The historical chain of use of the Gordon's building (901 Ryan Street) is instructive and offers a good example of the nature of business growth and development in downtown Lake Charles. In 1869, the site started modestly with a one-story wood building that housed Moss and Riddick General Merchandise, which catered to the young city's needs. In 1880, that one-story

This period picture shows the Gordon and Von Phul Drugstore and the mortar and pestle that long identified the structure. *Courtesy McNeese University Archives.*

building was replaced by the two-story, wood-framed D'Armond Building, which housed the Knapp Drug Store and the Hirsch Clothing Store. By 1897, Frank Von Phul and S.W. Gordon erected an imposing two-story, brick commercial building on the site to serve their pharmacy partnership and real estate possibilities. The site was one block from the courthouse and city hall; the two streetcar lines ran just outside the door; and the lakefront was a block to the west. Literally, it was the center of Lake Charles.

Directly on the corner of Ryan and Pujo was a huge mortar-and-pestle sculpture on a pedestal that used to advertise the Gordon Drug Store on the ground floor of the building. The second floor was used for professional and medical offices. The Pujo and Ryan intersection was one of the most important crossroads in town, with a high concentration of shops, theaters, banks, government and professional offices and hotels within a three-block radius. Significantly, Gordon's Drugs was one of the few pre-twentieth-century structures of brick in a town largely built of wood. A handsome annex of glazed brick and terra-cotta was constructed directly behind Gordon's and offered storefronts and upper-floor offices with Pujo Street addresses.

By the 1950s, drugstores in suburban locations had become more popular and the local chain of Gordon Drug Stores had closed its flagship downtown store. Sol Riff remodeled and relocated Riff's Palais Royal to this building. The Riff's store had been established in 1930 at 727 Ryan Street and, by 1955, had outgrown that site and moved to what had been Gordon's. The entire ground floor of the 901 building served as sales rooms for the upscale ladies' wear shop. In 1975, Riff's store relocated to an entirely new location designed for it in Southgate Shopping Center, a midcity shopping center on Ryan Street. (Since then, Riff's has ceased operations.) The 901 Ryan Building then became the home of the Boling Insurance Agency. Boling, established in the early 1950s, relocated from its offices on the ground floor of the Pioneer Building at 326 Pujo Street. In 1986, the Boling Agency merged with Insurance Unlimited. The agency expanded to offices on Prien Lake Road and closed its downtown offices. The building had been abandoned for some time when it was purchased by Shearman Properties in the early 1990s. Extensive rehabilitation work converted abandoned second-floor spaces to apartments and lofts. The ground floor was adaptively reused into restaurant space and serves as the current home of Pujo Street Café.

Within fifty years of founding and naming the city, there were hundreds of downtown buildings, shops, homes, banks, livery stables, theaters,

Turn-of-the-century Lake Charles as imaged on a postcard shows the tree-covered shores of the lake and the compact wood city that had grown up around the water. *Courtesy McNeese University Archives.*

vaudeville houses, hotels, churches, laundries and offices. Most were constructed of the readily available pine and cypress harvested and processed in the various civic sawmills. Balloon-framed buildings made use of readily available dimensional lumber, and roofs were sheathed in cypress shingles. Dozens of businesses jostled for trade along downtown streets with longtime staples like Martin's, Kaufmann's, Rouse Racket Store, the Williams Opera House, Rock Hardware, Rigmaiden Hotel, Lyric Theatre and dozens of other businesses proudly jostled for trade along downtown streets.

Brick structures were relatively few in number. The Majestic Hotel, opened in 1906, was constructed of brick and featured ceiling fans in every room along with its own water system and wells. The Gordon and Von Phul Drugstore, mentioned earlier, was built of brick and its annex of glazed brick. The Calcasieu State Bank, the Sunset Hotel, the train stations and a handful of other buildings were brick. But the bulk of downtown, including business, boardinghouses, shops and offices, were made of local richly pitched pine and cypress. Even roofs were made of flammable shingles, the least expensive and most available roofing material. Many of the elevated sidewalks were made of wood, as were storage buildings, fences and cisterns. Rapid growth had made for a compact city of wood—and, of course, wood was the preferred method for heating and cooking. Open fires were a common means for disposal of waste and to control mosquitoes. Literally, Lake Charles was a torch waiting to be lit.

# 4
# THE GREAT FIRE

## The Great Fire

It was a sunny, windy and hot Saturday morning on April 23, 1910, in Lake Charles. On the lake, cypress and pine logs floated in booms, awaiting the wranglers to skid them on land for processing. Buskers and traveling salesmen exchanged stories over biscuits and coffee in cafés and boardinghouses. Women were shopping for items for their Sunday dinners. Children were doing chores, working for a living, fishing or perhaps just playing hoops outside. It was an exciting time of fresh comings and goings with ferries and streetcars and trains. It was now just a breezy eight hours to New Orleans, with as many as twelve trains a day making runs. Just think of it!

Even with all this activity and energy, Lake Charles was generally a quiet southern town of about fifteen thousand. Electricity, gas, ice service and piped-in water were new and popular services of Gulf States Utilities, and the telegraph and telephone were well established and well used. The new St. Patrick's sanitarium had opened south of town a few years earlier. The city's public schools were operating with a wood Central School high school on the far edge of town, and one-room schoolhouses were scattered in various neighborhoods.

Both the city and parish had recently enlarged their modest seats of government. For the parish, a brick-and-wood courthouse annex had been erected in 1902 just to the east of the earlier courthouse and connected to it,

Sailing vessels were used on the lake and rivers until well into the twentieth century. *Courtesy McNeese University Archives.*

forming a long, thin, serviceable but somewhat confused-looking structure. The city had built its first city hall in 1903 facing Kirby Street at Cole. Before that, the city council met at homes, taverns, hotels and even on the second floor of the city's modest fire station.

Lake Charles served as the center of commerce for the immense Imperial Calcasieu Parish. Even though the ambitious real estate frenzy created by J.B. Watkins had brought thousands to southwest Louisiana, and Lake Charles was the center for that frenzy, most of the new settlers were dispersed on the wide Calcasieu Prairie lands, where they grew rice and cattle and built small farm-centered communities like Iowa, Kinder and Vinton. The Watkins vision of southwest Louisiana was essentially that of a rural paradise, not an urban one. Towns were built to serve the country, not the other way around.

Lake Charles was relatively compact in size. The entire city was defined by the lake and river on the west, Pithon Coulee on the south, Boulevard (now Enterprise Boulevard) on the east and rowdy Railroad Avenue (the

The St. Clair House was the height of hospitality in the nineteenth century. Note the open ditches crossed by the occasional wood bridges and the extensive use of wood, including wood shingles. *Courtesy the Imperial Calcasieu Museum.*

gateway to Goosport) on the north. In this compact community were some 350 buildings on Ryan Street alone. Even the new city hall shared a busy downtown block with the fire station, a livery stable and an assortment of businesses and homes on its small block.

It was a Saturday, a working day for most people. Men toiled at the mills or for the railroad, or they labored in shops and forges, warehouses, fields or, in rare cases, offices. Women maintained households, doing laundry, cleaning, cooking, baking and sewing. A few women operated their own shops and stores, but women-owned or operated businesses were few in number. Children would help their families with simple chores like harvesting vegetables from family gardens, collecting eggs, cleaning lamps or making beds. For working children, and there were many, the day meant running errands and delivering messages, helping in a shop, working for a blacksmith or a livery stable or, most dangerously, working at a sawmill or a in woodworking shop.

The few who worked a half day or, indeed, had the entire day off, might have taken one of the streetcars to Barbe's Pleasure Pier or to Walnut Grove to enjoy the day at a site where one could fish, swim or just hold hands at the water's edge. They might have chosen to visit friends or family, or perhaps they packed a picnic to enjoy at Orange Grove Cemetery. A lucky few might have chosen to take a short train excursion to visit the towns of Welsh or Jennings, or to Orange, Texas, and marvel at trains that raced at speeds of sixty miles per hour.

At 3:40 in the afternoon on April 23, 1910, Horton Porter, owner of Blaske's Soft Drink Stand (or, as it was more commonly known, the Old Opera House Saloon), and a young boy named Chaffin who ran errands for Gunn's Bookstore next door noticed a small, unattended trash fire behind the Williams Opera House. The young boy immediately began to throw water to quench the flame, and Porter ran to the fire department. According to the *American Press* newspaper of the day, Luther Sudduth, the fire chief, led the first wagon to the scene.

This view is looking south on Ryan Street toward the courthouse and Public Square early in the fire. Note the double line of streetcar tracks. Calcasieu State Bank and the Gordon and Von Phul Drugstore are at left. *Courtesy McNeese University Archives.*

The Hazel was the cross-lake ferry at the time of the fire and provided one means of escaping the inferno. However, as the fire grew, the vessel was forced to remain on the western shore. *Courtesy MSU Archives.*

Within fifteen minutes, the fire ballooned out, fanned by the gale-force winds off the lake. The opera house was engulfed by burning embers. Wood outbuildings, fences and scrub trees were ignited, as well. The opera house had been built of heart pine, which is rich in pitch and tar. The floors of the facility, like most wooden floors of the era, were regularly oiled and waxed to keep them clean. Buildings were densely connected and had common walls. Some buildings were linked by wood banquettes and awnings. Most had shingled roofs. All this dry wood, along with the strong winds, made fighting the fire a dangerous and difficult task.

The opera house was soon a furnace. The *American Press* reported that the firefighters and volunteers directed "four streams of water on the blaze which came down as steam from the intense heat." A black, billowing cloud of smoke rose from the flames, and embers crackled down on adjacent buildings on both sides of the 900 block of Ryan Street. The fire ignited the Catholic church, a wood structure. Soon, the rectory, convent and school on the east side of Ryan Street blazed, as well.

Additional fire hoses and pumps were brought in from the sawmills, and more men volunteered to fight the flames with blankets and buckets.

The opera house exploded in a torrent of embers. The shower of embers leapt North Court Street and landed on the wood window casings of the courthouse. Firefighters scrambled to both fight the expanding fire and evacuate the buildings. Parish employees tried to save the records and furniture. Susan Bilbo McNeese, wife of longtime school superintendent John McNeese, who was out of town that day, famously rushed to the courthouse to pitch school records out of the windows to workers on the ground. Many other records of criminal and civil cases, court proceedings and property records were destroyed as the courthouse and annex were engulfed and leveled by fire.

In another ninety minutes, the wind had spread the inferno from its start in the 900 block of Ryan to as far north as Division Street, as far south as Clarence Street and as far east as Kirkman Street. A total of 109 buildings were in the immediate path of the flames. As the amount of generated smoke, flying embers and flame grew, alarm grew, and the entire city prepared for a major conflagration. The ferries connecting the lakefront with Westlake and the other communities were halted on the opposite shore with panicked passengers. Fire whistles blew the alarm at the few fire stations throughout town, at lumber mills and factories all along the lake. Church bells rang

This 1903 image shows the long, thin courthouse that fell victim to the great fire. *Courtesy McNeese University Archives.*

throughout the city to spread the alarm. Railroad bells and whistles shrilly proclaimed the conflagration throughout the city. By five o'clock, the din of sirens, bells and mill whistles was continuous.

Individuals and families who feared that their homes could be next evacuated with household goods and furnishings. Some used horses and wagons, others the still-working streetcars. A few families placed household goods on the street in an effort to save them from house flames, and there are family tales of the house being saved while the furnishings in the street caught fire from errant embers. The members of the Christian church, then located on Iris Street, removed their cherished new organ and placed it on the street for safekeeping. Unfortunately, both it and the church were consumed in flames. Interestingly, but sadly, the congregants later discovered that had they kept the organ in the church, it would have been covered by their fire insurance along with the building!

A gusting wind from the southwest blew embers and smoke across Ryan Street and to the north and east. Even distant business proprietors and homeowners wet quilts and blankets and used them to smother ground flames and spot fires. Using steam-powered pumps that drew water from the lake as well as from hydrants, firemen attempted to squelch flames on roofs and porches in the congested downtown.

Horses were led out of burning stables and herded to safety lakeside or across Pithon Coulee. Merchandise was carted away, and residents emptied their houses to try to save family heirlooms. The jail was emptied, and inmates were drafted to help fight the fire. A fire line had been established at Common Street, and dynamite was used to help clear firebreaks.

Directly in the path of the fire were buildings on Pujo Street between Hodges and the waterfront. The Carnegie library, the Majestic Hotel, the Calcasieu State Bank and the Gordon Drug Store building and annex were all targets. All these structures were brick, but wood had also been used in their construction. As the great fire spewed a continuing shower of burning embers over the city, employees of the Majestic Hotel sprayed water nonstop on the roofs and sides of these neighboring buildings in a successful effort to protect lives, property and contents. The Majestic saved those structures and, in doing so, saved itself. After the fire, the Majestic provided housing for some of the displaced citizens and served as temporary city and parish staging areas, allowing business to be conducted until new facilities were constructed.

The Majestic Hotel had been built in 1906 to be the modern ultimate hotel for Lake Charles. The area had many lesser hotels and

Built in 1906, the Majestic Hotel boasted all the latest features, including ceiling fans in every room, private bathrooms and an updated water system. It was torn down in the mid-1960s. *Courtesy McNeese University Archives.*

boardinghouses in its day, such as the Haskell House, the St. Clair and the Lake House. The Majestic was bigger and grander. It had its own power plant and water system, as well as ceiling fans in every guestroom. It had a popular restaurant and was alleged to have hosted every president from Theodore Roosevelt to John F. Kennedy, though not necessarily when they were president.

The fire continued to burn eastward and southward. Continuous destruction ended at the Catholic Cemetery at Iris and Common Streets and arced north and westward. However, windblown embers caused spot fires in much of the rest of the city. A house located six full blocks away on Kirkman Street ignited and went up in flames. Similarly, spot fires were reported throughout the city, the result of embers landing on dry shingle roofs. It was a long and difficult night, with most citizens wary of burning embers from the desiccated and smoke-filled sky.

Pithon Coulee kept the fire from progressing any farther south along Ryan Street. At the time, the coulee was graced with what amounted to a large freshwater cypress-and-tupelo swamp at the foot of Front Street (now Lakeshore Drive) where it joined Clarence Street. The swamp kept the fire from progressing into Margaret Perkins's farm on the other shore. Before the construction of Shell Beach Road, a rickety boardwalk crossed the coulee to the south shore of the lake. The boardwalk was known as a local "lover's lane" for its unchaperoned use by young couples. There are period postcards of this notorious landmark.

On the north side, flames continued almost to Division Street; on the northeast, the strong southwest wind fanned the flames almost to Kirkman Street. Over thirty blocks of the city were affected; seven whole city blocks were burned to the ground. About a third of the population of Lake Charles was made homeless. Many were temporarily housed in commodity warehouses along Railroad Avenue, in the homes of friends and relatives in other parts of the city and in churches. The rice mills provided cauldrons of boiled rice in an effort to allay hunger.

Once the fire expanded beyond the relatively dense downtown, where roofs and walls were made of wood, the lack of fuel literally killed the fire. In less than five hours, the Great Fire of 1910 turned a downtown of pine and cypress into heaps of smoldering ash.

## From the Ashes

Essential to the general survival of the area was the return of order; the reconstruction of city hall, the courthouse and the jail; and the reestablishment of the many businesses and homes that had been lost. In addition, documented parish, business and church records had to be reconstructed. The *New York Times* reported that the fire made five thousand people homeless and destroyed some $4 million worth of real estate alone. To give an idea of the value in today's money: at the time, a well-appointed three-bedroom house cost well under $2,000, and a gallon of gasoline cost $0.07.

The effort to reconstruct parish land records took more than twelve months, and many land abstracts to this day begin with the words "on the 23rd of April, 1910, a great conflagration" to explain some of the inconsistencies in tracking ownership. While the staff at the clerk of court is generally helpful and conscientious, some requests for specific documents from the period get the response, "Oh, dear, that was burned up in the fire."

Despite the great loss of property and records, there was no known loss of life as a result of the fire, except for one unfortunate temporary guest of the parish sheriff. The jail had been lost in the fire, and the jailer of

The extent of loss is evident in this image from the turret of the Calcasieu State Bank Building, looking southwest. All that was left were ashes. *Courtesy McNeese University Archives.*

Calcasieu Parish, son of a sheriff and part of the great Reid family dynasty of Calcasieu lawmen, determined that his prisoners would remain prisoners for the duration of their sentence.

Jailer J.D. Reid transported the prisoners to his own home at Ford and Pine Streets, where they resided as his guests for about a year. Local lore has it that during this time, one of the prisoners attempted an escape from the third-floor attic, where the temporary jail had been established. The escape, attempted by crashing through the attic's window, failed. As the tale continues, the ghostly sounds of breaking glass and a last desperate cry are sometimes heard in the neighborhood on moonless evenings.

Another casualty of the fire may have been Imperial Calcasieu Parish itself. Calcasieu Parish had been created in 1840 from the western half of St. Landry Parish. Thirty years later, Cameron Parish was carved out of the coastal part of Calcasieu with its own courthouse and traditions. By the end of the century, communities in the eastern and northern parts of Calcasieu Parish had begun petitioning to establish their own parishes and courts.

Residents of the Merryville and DeRidder areas held at least two formal convocations to petition independence from Calcasieu Parish as early as 1900. For property transfers, tax payments, jury duty and other necessary court business, residents had to make an overnight trip to the parish seat of Lake Charles by horse or train.

The loss of records may have tipped the scales in the movement to establish new parishes. Seven months after the fire, a special convention of the ten wards of Imperial Calcasieu Parish was called with the specific purpose of formally dividing up old Calcasieu Parish; by 1912, the civil parishes of Jefferson Davis, Allen and Beauregard, the last three civil parishes of Louisiana, were carved out and established.

Not only did the fire clear out the early and, in some cases, original development in downtown Lake Charles, it also cleared out the almost medieval notion of how cities work. The European, colonial and early American model of towns and cities was unplanned, with little regard for safety. Structures were quickly run up from materials at hand—wood here in Lake Charles—and most buildings were utilitarian in purpose, undistinguished in appearance; sometimes, only a crudely crafted sign distinguished a barbershop from a boardinghouse. Recovery from the Great Fire of 1910 included a completely new, modern way of building and using downtown spaces and facilities. A twentieth-century city of space, symbol and utility would be crafted.

The fire had been so intense and complete that there was little left to restore. Photographs documenting the fire show a bleak landscape of little more than fire-damaged chimneys. The civic slate had been literally washed clean by the fire. Both the police jury and city council decided early on to tackle recovery from several different angles at once. Immediately following the fire, the need for security was primary. The state militia, sheriff's department and city police maintained around-the-clock watches on the lookout for looting and other misconduct. The fire department went on special alert to monitor errant blazes from the hundreds of piles of ashes and rubble.

Revised, updated building codes were soon in place following a short moratorium on all types of construction in downtown. Fire codes and lists of suitable building materials, styles and setbacks were reviewed and put into place. Missing city and parish documents were reconstructed from bits of existing records and from memory. Abstractors, realtors, clerks, lawyers, judges and common folk literally testified to reconstruct some records, some based on witnessing events and from diaries, mortgages, family Bibles and personal notes of civil and criminal records. It took well over a year to reconstitute practically all property records and successions using materials that had been in the temporary care of an abstracting company located away from the fire along with other sources.

The actions of the paid fire department were reviewed critically, as was the availability of hydrants and water pressure. Fire Chief Sudduth was fired, but the water company review passed muster as providing sufficient water pressure. Streets were cleared, and the streetcar lines and utilities systems were reestablished in record time. The fire was deemed a natural disaster—an act of God—and blame and censure was not issued. Given the dry gale-force winds and the unregulated, densely packed city of wood, it was the only sane conclusion.

One of the early post-fire decisions was to abandon the alderman-mayor format of civic government. By 1912, Lake Charles began to operate on a commission basis, considered then to be a more modern, more progressive, business-like approach to civic government. The commission form was promoted as encouraging sound fiscal practice and rejecting waste and favoritism. This form presided over the next two decades of rapid civic growth and improvement. In many respects, the city had matured and began to think of itself as a modern city, rather than as just a sawmill outpost or cow town. Lake Charles finally viewed itself worthy of all possibilities. To a great extent, the average citizen, most elected officials and many city leaders viewed Lake Charles the same way that many of the immigrants and newcomers to the community had envisioned it a generation earlier: a city of promise and limitless potential.

# 5
# THE TWENTIETH CENTURY

## Favrot and Livaudais; Form and Substance

The decision to reconstruct downtown exactly where it had once stood was a simple and popular one. The decision to build better was made evident by the unusual, apparently coincidental selection of the prestigious New Orleans–based architectural firm of Favrot and Livaudais for the three principal commissions to replace lost public buildings. Previously, nearly all homes and most commercial buildings were constructed using pattern books by talented carpenter-builders. In a city of sawmills, most structures had been utilitarian in form, ornamented by saw-cut gingerbread possibly, and certainly made of the most easily procured building material: wood. Professionally designed and engineered structures were nearly non-existent, except possibly for the railroad stations, which used an engineered template provided directly by the railroad company.

Favrot and Livaudais was a long-established architectural and engineering firm with many civic, academic and religious commissions throughout the South, the East Coast and the Midwest to its credit. In designing for this area's particular needs and conservative approach to life in general, the firm used traditional building styles, academically based, but it shaped the interiors for modern practical use. Strong and distinctive historically based exteriors provided the big-picture symbolism. As for the interiors, they would be shaped by beauty, function and utility. And, of course, the firm selected

This is a current view of the 1911 city hall, the first of Favrot and Livaudais's visions of a new Lake Charles downtown built on the ashes of the old. *From the author's collection.*

brick, marble, terra-cotta, copper, bronze, tile and other fireproof materials that have stood the test of time.

The first commission completed was for the new city hall. The completed building is Italianate in style with a central clock tower and fireproof tile roof. The design placed city hall facing Ryan Street and surrounded by spacious, terraced grounds covering the entire block. No longer was city hall mired in an area chockablock with wood-frame structures.

Across Ryan Street, the city abandoned South Court Street to provide more grounds for the new parish courthouse to be surrounded by a park-like square. Here, Favrot and Livaudais used the classic Palladian style with columns, porticos and a massive copper dome—a traditional building enveloping the heart of modern parish government and the courts. The principal façade faced Ryan Street to the east and saluted the new city hall almost directly across the way. There were once equally impressive courthouse entrances on the north, west and south, as well, but these façades are now obscured by later additions. The designed new courthouse was (and is) classic, pure, elegant and at the same time approachable and grand.

These two important buildings were monumental in scale and designed to inspire and edify the common man and woman. They were built to serve for centuries. They were to act as vessels for the business conducted within the structure, and they served as the symbol of that activity. They reflected the belief of the importance of good government, conservative wisdom and the stewardship of resources. The functions of city and parish government were elevated, both literally and figuratively, as the main entrances are not set on the street level—the level of the ordinary and of the everyday. Government functions were made special by elevating them, both symbolically and physically. The spaces and details are grand, and the materials used are solid and real, to allow the structures to withstand hard daily use and to impress both citizen and visitor. The buildings became the symbols of Calcasieu and Lake Charles and represent strength, wisdom, prudence and tradition. They are well-loved buildings today. (Today, most people enter these two grand buildings from the rear, ground-level entrances and use the grand ceremonial entrances only on special occasions.)

A symbol of the parish, the great copper dome of the Calcasieu Courthouse shelters the activities of many parish offices. *From the author's collection.*

Of particular concern to the Catholics of the parish was the loss of their 1881 wood-framed church, which had replaced the first modest church built in 1869. By 1910, the congregation had added a rectory, a convent and a school, which provided education to day students and to boarders who lived at the convent. The entire complex had been leveled by the fire. It was the only Catholic church to serve a region of over five thousand square miles.

To replace the Catholic church and rectory, Favrot and Livaudais chose the Romanesque-Lombard basilica style, but in a deep red brick rather than in stucco. The new Immaculate Conception Church followed a classical outline with rounded arched windows and a distinctive bell tower. Later, a new convent and school, St. Charles Academy, would be constructed at a respectful distance from downtown in the new Margaret Place development. St. Charles Academy is now demolished, but the Cathedral Church of the Immaculate Conception is a striking landmark of the city and of the congregation it serves.

In all, three remarkable, diverse and striking downtown landmarks are the architectural souvenirs of the robust recovery from the great fire. Each of the three is now individually listed in the National Register of Historic Places. These buildings are arguably the most significant architecture ever built in southwest Louisiana. They are the physical evidence of a determined decision to build bigger and better after a challenging disaster.

Later, businesses and private citizens commissioned the Favrot and Livaudais firm for additional new structures in Lake Charles, including Lock Park Pavilion, several private homes and the Calcasieu Marine National Bank, to name a few. In addition, the new parish of Allen chose this firm to design a courthouse in Oberlin for the freshly minted parish.

Favrot and Livaudais were also responsible for the 1912 Central School, which replaced an earlier wood school on the same site. Three other matching but smaller primary schools were also built at that time. The First, Second and Fourth Ward Schools were all demolished when they were deemed obsolete. But Central, also known as Third Ward, was not only saved from possible demolition, it was also converted to a cultural center complete with learning centers, museums, a theater and artists' studios by the City of Lake Charles in the 1990s. In memory of its cherished service to the children of the community, the city voted to restore and reuse the building, purchasing it back from the Calcasieu Parish School System. For sixty years, Central had been a city school, like the ward schools, Lake Charles High and Boston High School, all run by and for the city.

When Central School was declared obsolete in the early 1990s, concerned citizens petitioned to use a temporary sales tax to purchase the structure and update it into a working center for the arts and humanities. *From the author's collection.*

For many of the families displaced by the fire, the choice to rebuild was not a difficult one. For a few families, like that of Judge Thomas Gorham, a new home was built exactly where the old one had been, in some cases using the same floor plan. Many families sold their old lots and selected new residential areas of town that were being developed as the streetcar lines were extended.

One such new development was Margaret Place, located on what had been the old Perkins Farm southwest of downtown. Other families took the opportunity to start fresh in the Broad Street area, which had long been popular, with both grand houses and cottages being constructed on the side streets. Farther south and east on what was the edge of town, new houses were being built around the Louisiana Baptist Orphanage and farms. What had been open prairie meadows was becoming the city. The saplings planted at these new homes have turned into the mature live oaks that grace those areas today.

## Flirting with Aviation

Five short years after the opening of the new courthouse designed to look at home in Renaissance Italy, the now forward-thinking city (and parish) competed nationally to host the construction of an Army Air Signal Corps training base. At the start of World War I, the U.S. Army realized that the nation was in no way prepared for possible participation in the growing conflict in Europe. While the conflict was viewed as Europe's war, many links connected the United States with England and France. The military wanted to be prepared.

The decade of experimental aviation that began with the Wright brothers firmly established the multiple military uses of aircraft. The city and the parish understood that there was intense public fascination with the various newly invented flying machines and recognized their possibilities and destructive power in war. In Lake Charles, there was the availability of year-round flying weather and flat, even land for runways. In addition, there was the energized support of business and civic leaders and of the general population. In a still largely agrarian area where most citizens used horses and mules, to actively engage in the pursuit of the cutting-edge airplane training bases was remarkable. In the presentation package advanced by the Association of Commerce were photographs of newly constructed "aeroplane bungalows," named for their slight resemblance to biplanes, with a large central dormer (cockpit) over a widespread porch (the wings). The claim was made that "aeroplanes" were all the rage in Lake Charles and that even the houses boasted cockpits.

Together, these factors made possible the construction of a double training facility that opened as Gerstner Air Field, the first military airfield established in Louisiana, located just south of the city. Gerstner had twenty-four hangars, ninety support structures and a rail connection to central Lake Charles. Almost five hundred fighter pilots and instructors trained here, including General Jimmy Doolittle, Captain Ernest Harmon, General Claire Chennault and Captain Maxwell Kirby, who is credited with downing the last enemy airplane in World War I. Aerial gunnery and wireless communication between ground and pilot, as well as airplane ambulance service, were pioneered at this airbase. The facility—designed to be temporary—was completely dismantled in 1921. Many of the still-usable buildings were salvaged and converted to farmhouses and barns. One of the officers' messes was removed to Lake Charles to serve as the assembly space for the Church of Christ, Scientist on Kirby Street (where it still stands). Signage marks the location of Gerstner Field. The runways and some of the foundations remain at the site, and the road connecting it to Lake Charles was named for the field. Other than that (and the odd repurposed building claiming to be from the decommissioned site), there is very little tangible evidence of Louisiana's first military airbase.

Gerstner Field made significant contributions to fighting World War I. In addition, the community's connections linked the airmen of Gerstner, while it existed, to Lake Charles. Servicemen were entertained by local hostesses, and the military participated in civic events, providing patriotic bands and engaging the community in the wonder and beauty of flight. From bombing practice on prairie fields marked with bull's-eye targets of lime and flour laid out by willing farmers to the dramatic aerial dogfights over rice fields witnessed by farmhands and cowboys, the existence of Gerstner Field engaged the imaginations and expanded the horizons of many a young man and woman in Lake Charles. A fondness for aviators and aviation was branded into the soul of southwest Louisiana.

With the rumblings of a second world war, the Parish Police Jury quickly leased the newly opened civilian Lake Charles Municipal Airport to the federal government for the Lake Charles Army Flying School. Advanced single-engine training continued there until 1943, when the facility was assigned to the Third Air Force as the Lake Charles Army Airfield. At the end of World War II, the airfield remained open and housed the Forty-Seventh Bombardment Group, which flew A-26 Invaders. In 1947, the airfield was closed and the site returned to the City of Lake Charles.

The Korean War reactivated the renamed Lake Charles Air Force Base in 1951. The facility was upgraded to SAC standards for B-29 Superfortress aircraft and included expanded runway length, hangar space and officer and staff accommodations. The base handled Boeing KC-97 Stratofreighters and other advanced jets. One of the longest runways in the world was constructed at the base to accommodate scheduled activities.

In 1958, the base was renamed for the late General Claire Chennault, who had trained at Gerstner Field more than forty years earlier. The base served as a Strategic Air Command (SAC) base until 1963, when it was officially deactivated and returned to local control for economic development purposes. That facility, Chennault International Airport, currently operates general aviation and maintenance, with constant major tenants over the last forty-five years providing thousands of jobs. In addition, the site provides for the expansive campus of SOWELA

Technical and Community College, which includes aviation maintenance and mechanics as part of its extensive catalogue of degrees, training options and course options.

## Extractive Industry and the Growth of Petrochem

In 1901, petroleum was first successfully produced in Louisiana north of Jennings, at that time part of Calcasieu Parish. Using local investment, a modest refinery opened to take advantage of the productive Jennings Field. Within a few years, wildcatters discovered deposits of oil and gas all over the parish, part of the birth of today's energy coast of Louisiana and Texas. By 1903, a modest locally financed refinery was located in Lake Charles.

While exploration and extraction were and are strong in the area, for Lake Charles, the focus was on refining and on various downstream industries.

This early aerial view of the Columbia-Southern plant, later PPG and now Axiall, suggests the complex interconnections that made the industrial corridor successful. *Courtesy McNeese University Archives.*

As lumbering and timber processing waned with sawmills following the industry north and west, investment in downstream petroleum refining and in petrochemical activities increased.

World War II was the major catalyst for extensive petrochemical investment in the Lake Charles area. Continental Oil (CONOCO) constructed a large refinery (now Phillips 66) just across the river from Lake Charles, soon followed by a state-of-the-art Cities Services refinery a little farther south. The unique juncture of resources, water access (via barge, port and intracoastal canal), pipeline and highways made for a powerhouse industrial combination on the western shore. The war effort was viewed as paramount, and competitors Cities Services and CONOCO collaborated on additional ventures for lubricating oil, distillates and other products, with the newly created Cit-Con plant being the first successful operation of the competing but cooperating refineries.

Building on the ready availability of land, resources and workforce, there are currently literally dozens of multinational and national corporations operating refineries, plants, transportation hubs and facilities, providing thousands of jobs in the downstream petroleum and related industries in the Lake Charles region. In the last ten years, the liquefied natural gas industry has boomed in the region, first with import facilities in place and now with several working exporting terminals in play along the shores of the Calcasieu Ship Channel.

The Italian monopoly on the production of sulfur had been broken with the creation of the Frasch method in nearby Sulphur, Louisiana, in the late nineteenth century. For several decades, this element, essential for many modern chemical processes, was commercially produced at the Brimstone Mines, giving the west Calcasieu community the nickname the "richest fifty acres in America." Sulfur produced in Calcasieu Parish was shipped by rail to the established deepwater port on the Sabine River to the west, a sour plum for Lake Charles. To some extent, this sour plum triggered an ongoing realization of the need for a true deepwater port with reliable connections to the open seas.

## THE PORT OF LAKE CHARLES

National objectives to provide protected barge access along the Gulf and Atlantic coasts began in earnest as early as the mid-nineteenth century. But it took until 1924 for an inland waterways act to make the Intracoastal Canal

Prior to deepwater access, sailing schooners were extensively used, like this one. A cargo of Cameron Parish citrus is being unloaded at a private dock in the 1920s. *Courtesy McNeese University Archives.*

possible. This waterway was designed to provide a man-made protected channel through marshes and prairie and to improve coastal bays, inlets and sounds to allow for year-round bulk cargo barges. Barges were long the most cost-effective means of extremely heavy transport, and barge access and this waterway was planned to link the entire Gulf and Atlantic coastline. (Interestingly, the principal champion for the Intracoastal was one-time mayor of Lake Charles Leon Locke, sometimes called the "father of the Intracoastal.) The Intracoastal would allow for better access of barge traffic from Lake Charles east and west.

The barge traffic link to the wharves and commerce of Lake Charles was important. But much more significant to long-term growth was that direct deepwater access to the Gulf. The sulfur industry had used the Sabine as its preferred means of shipping. The operating steamers and sailing schooners made do with an unreliable and shallow lower Calcasieu River. There were longstanding issues with the shoals at its mouth. (One of the first steamers built here, the *Dan*, a product of Goos Shipyard, was specifically built to tow schooners over those very shoals.). In early sailing days, unpredictable winds could turn simple excursions into days of waiting or rowing. The perishable agricultural products of rice and cattle, and promising new cargoes of oil and petrochemicals, could only expand to the extent that transportation options could both accommodate the volume and guarantee deadlines.

Between 1921 and 1924, without any federal or state assistance, local citizens engineered and built a seaport that would first access the Sabine River and the Intracoastal Waterway. To connect the various modes of transport, Lake Charles had to create ready and dependable access to the Gulf. It did this by actually re-shaping the river, straightening the course of the lower Calcasieu River, cutting through a series of horseshoe bends and dredging the shallow lagoon-like lakes to shorten and deepen the route to the Gulf. When state and federal funding did not materialize, local citizens took action independently. The City Docks of the Port of Lake Charles opened in 1926, and the ship channel was completed

Reliable access to both deep water and the Intracoastal Waterway was made possible by the construction of City Docks, shown here in progress in 1925. *Courtesy McNeese University Archives.*

by 1941. Both are managed by the Port of Lake Charles Commission, which also, to a great extent, controls the activities on the man-made and natural banks of the waterway.

If you look at a map of the Calcasieu River area, you can see the islands created by this long-term process. Channelization allowed for oceangoing vessels to come up directly to Lake Charles's commercial docks, and this one act most certainly encouraged the industrial growth of the entire area. Deepwater access and protected berths allow cargo to be transferred from oceangoing vessels to barges for the Intracoastal, or to rail, to tank farms, to pipelines or to highway traffic, and vice versa. Industry, shipping companies, construction contractors and even the hospitality and casino industries are reliant on port resources for their facilities and success.

But the channelization that created the port also allowed Gulf salt water to ebb and flow up the channel, an action that allowed for salt water to migrate upstream, eventually killing off the cypress that once grew so proficiently in the river and lakes. Early images of Prien Lake, Lake Charles and Moss Lake show extensive cypress and tupelo in the waters that were fresh at that point; the waters soon become brackish. A control structure (the Salt Water Barrier) just north of the city of Lake Charles prevents salt water from migrating even farther northward. However, it is still possible to fish for both saltwater and freshwater fish in some of the lakes. From the Lakeshore Promenade at the Lake Charles Civic Center one can land redfish and sheepshead (both native to offshore waters), as well as bass and bream (from upstream freshwater).

Significantly, channelization also allows for storm surge to affect populated areas as much as forty miles from the coast. These shoreline areas had been protected for millennia by those twisty bends and oxbows of the early Calcasieu that dampened and diverted the energy of storm surge. Ironically, the freshwater environment that grew the cypress—the product that was first carried by the schooner trade and later carried by steam and diesel—would be destroyed by the inevitable growth of that very shipping trade. Channelization created the port boom and makes many things possible in a richly industrialized Lake Charles, but that channelization process also positions Lake Charles, and with it much of the prosperity of southwest Louisiana, on a knife-edge of exposure to storm surge, saltwater intrusion and erosion.

The final dredging of the new Calcasieu Ship Channel in 1941 shortened the physical distance from the docks to the open Gulf, from more than seventy-five miles to just thirty-three, a distance that makes the Port of Lake

A 1930s image of a ship at the new Port of Lake Charles. During the Depression, the port was a rare source of sought-after jobs. *Courtesy McNeese University Archives.*

Charles one of the nearest major ports to open waters. In addition, the port promotes and leases the adjacent lands, which have been used for a variety of industrial purposes, for transportation hubs, for recreation and fishing and even for upscale casino resorts.

The establishment of the port provided the essential logistics catalyst for major chemical industrialization of the area, industrialization primarily centered on the western shore. Even with the worldwide depression in 1933, the first industrial player on water frontage, Mathieson Alkali Works, was successfully financed and constructed. Production of ammonia-soda and caustic soda was in place there by early 1935, to be followed by a chain of industrial ventures on adjacent land. In the early war years, state-of-the-art refineries and petrochemical plants were successfully constructed and operated as part of the war effort. Later facilities that made use of byproducts or refined and reworked other products followed. This chain of industrial productivity and innovation has continued unbroken for nearly eighty years, with various national and international companies making investments, as well.

From the opening of the port, through the Depression years, through completion of the channel and through World War II, Lake Charles

In 1957, the port provided staging for the rescue of the victims of Hurricane Audrey, which devastated Cameron Parish. Here, ambulances are lined up on the docks to assist with the effort. *Courtesy McNeese University Archives.*

hummed with a variety of major business ventures that served as a regional magnet, providing opportunity and jobs. While the local lumber industry was ending its days as a major player, there were still trees to the north to be cut and stumps to be processed for turpentine. In the waning days of the lumber industry, when some sawmill components and equipment ended their productive lives in southwest Louisiana, they were shipped out via the port to areas of more promise.

The rice industry was also galvanized by increased market demand, advances in production and new (and cheaper) access to world markets. The regional cattle industry had opened a major new meatpacking facility, the Swift Plant, which began production in earnest in 1937. The 1920s turned into the working 1930s, which then passed to the war effort of the 1940s. The refineries were productive. The port was prospering, rail was still strong, a new junior college and a new vocational-technical school had opened, unions were training craftsmen and Lake Charles was a magnet for workers from throughout the South. A promise of continued prosperity was in the air.

# 6
# CRAFTING A FUTURE

## SUBURBANIZATION

The growth of industry in the area, occurring at the same time as the Depression and the war years were negatively affecting much of the rest of America, made Lake Charles and southwest Louisiana a market for jobseekers in the 1930s, '40s and early '50s. The city grew with temporary construction workers, permanent workers and servicemen at the airbase. During this time, the training and job security offered by unions occasionally abraded capital investment and plant management, and vice versa. In addition, workers were drawn here as part of the booming economy as the community expanded rapidly to provide housing, markets, restaurants, shops, movie houses, healthcare, education and all the other goods and services needed for a modern, expanding city.

Traditional neighborhoods and villages began to change, and new areas, some developed from what had been farmland, began to be created. New subdivisions developed along existing roadways. New businesses lined the appropriately named South Street (later renamed Ryan Street), which went south and west and became the road to the Lake Charles Country Club. The part of South Ryan Street (now Dr. Michael DeBakey Drive) ran parallel to the south shore of Lake Charles and made a left turn south to become Lake Street. Common Street became the Gulf Highway on its journey to connect to the communities of Sweetlake and beyond. Prien Lake Road and

Opelousas Street led to the countryside, as did U.S. Highways 90 and 171 and Louisiana Highway 14. Each of these country roads provided a basis for new development along its length, with neighborhoods created on cross streets and side roads. Suburbanization had begun in earnest.

The ideal home for suburban Lake Charles was new, built on a slab of concrete, with a front yard, backyard and a garage or carport—essentially the suburban standard for all of postwar America. The proud owner might work at one of the plants or for a contractor; his wife might be a homemaker or, later in the period, work out of the home at a bank or office. The average couple had two and a half children. The workweek was Monday through Friday, and shift work was the norm for blue-collar workers. The weekends were for sports and hobbies and for church. This was the working social contract of postwar America, successful to a large degree for fifty years. Unfortunately, this was not a one-size-fits-all model. Economic and social diversity had not been factored in completely. But for many citizens of Lake Charles, it was a fine working model.

Lake Charles has two good examples of how suburbs have physically changed in the past seventy-five years to meet the differing social and economic needs of those generations. The suburbs that best characterize those changes are Oak Park and Graywood.

Really more of a village, Oak Park was the American Dream, albeit Lake Charles–style, and relatively advanced for its day. For about thirty years, Oak Park was one of the most coveted addresses in southwest Louisiana. Covering a large part of the city, with avenue and numbered-street addresses, the very popular development offered a tailored, urbane approach to suburban life. Somewhat closer to the center of the city than most subdivisions, Oak Park was well positioned in terms of offering access to schools, jobs, shops and services.

A development project of the local Huber family, Oak Park's long and ordered history focused on providing housing and a true community atmosphere in what amounts to a controlled park-like setting. It was developed in stages and covers more than one hundred city blocks. The grid features thousands of live oak trees, planted to provide shade and shelter on what had been the Calcasieu prairie. One of the early claims of advertisements for Oak Park was cooling shade for every homeowner—no small feat in an era before the common use of air-conditioning. Even today, the number of still-existing trees on the development is in excess of two thousand, one of the largest planned groves of live oaks anywhere on earth. Oak Park Boulevard was to be the commercial and retail core for a complete

This is an early view of Memorial Hospital on Oak Park Boulevard at Second Avenue. Today, the original building has been entirely encapsulated by the hospital's growth. *Courtesy McNeese University Archives.*

community. The development was the location of a healthcare "village" that included (and still includes) Lake Charles Memorial Hospital, many private doctors and clinics and other allied health specialists. The development also had dedicated elementary and middle schools, shops and stores, churches, service alleyways, parks and playgrounds and even gateway markers that said you had arrived.

In far southwest Lake Charles, Graywood, a village of subdivisions under development, uses many similar but updated land-use concepts. High-end features include a mix of parkland, golf course, strict construction covenants and a high regard for aesthetics. The development is defined by limited-access neighborhoods with curving roadways, cul-de-sacs and an emphasis on vista and neighborhood. Graywood, much more land-conscious than Oak Park, is designed to shape itself to its unique water's-edge location rather than by imposing an artificial, regimented grid regardless of terrain conditions, as with Oak Park.

However, Graywood does not seem to provide to any extent space for live-work scenarios, retail, service, mixed-use or professional needs. Its mission is to focus on the high-end mix of residential with leisure and resort amenities, a thoroughly millennial concept. This luxury does come at a cost, both economically—home prices tend to be high—and in its relatively remote location from standard city services, hospitals, jobs, entertainment and schools. Graywood is perhaps the largest of the many subdivisions in south Lake Charles and certainly a catalyst for new commercial development in that area.

## Popular Culture

A mixture of influences from many cultures, countries and tastes has shaped the creativity and popular culture of Lake Charles. Any history must examine the areas of culture, leisure and recreation in order to better provide a picture of what makes a good place to live and work. Since the first days of settlement, and all through the 150-year history of the city, the way people spend their leisure hours is telling. In some cases, leisure activities have developed into their own significant industries.

Recreational hunting and fishing have evolved from the early survival aspects of life on the marshes, prairies and woodland to today's specialized sports, industries of their own. Hunting and fishing are very nearly bred into the DNA of the area. Both locals and tourists avail themselves of the rich opportunities of hunting and fishing camps, tournaments and the several seasons that offer sport (and, for most, a source of consumable game) at sites just outside the city limits. Hunting and fishing, along with bird watching and wildlife photography, have also been integrated into the wider community with solid connections to ecology and conservation efforts. Many nonprofit social services are supported by fishing and hunting fundraisers, and even cuisine has developed that uses the unique game and fish of the area. The vast wild areas that surround Lake Charles offer unique opportunities to commune with an earlier, simpler America.

Every water-based city has a history of pleasure boating, water sports and swimming, and Lake Charles is no exception. Access to water has been directly connected to the unique history and heritage of the area. The abundant resources of freshwater and salt water meant that many families had and cared for vessels from the very first settlement of the area. Boat ownership, like history itself, starts with simple pirogues, rowboats and bateaux. Today, it extends to sailboats, catamarans, cabin cruisers and even yachts.

A day on the water in Lake Charles means a day of relaxation and renewal. Popular areas for day excursions include the upper Calcasieu River, the west fork and Houston River, English Bayou, Contraband Bayou, the actual Lake Charles, Indian Bay, Prien Lake and Moss Lake, all on the city's edges. There are hundreds of spots, coves and inlets that provide that special place for fun on the water.

In early Lake Charles, pure edification and cultural entertainment came from vaudeville houses, theaters, bandstands and pleasure piers that offered a range of concerts, balls, animal acts, dramatic readings, comedians and even the occasional legitimate theater. Professional acts and events proliferated once the railroads connected the young city with the rest of America. In the early part of the twentieth century, the particular site of Lake Charles on the rail line between the giant entertainment-consuming communities of New Orleans and Houston made for an interesting scheduling activity: the Sunday show.

The way the Sunday show played out was that professional entertainment acts would schedule closing nights in New Orleans theaters, clubs and vaudeville houses on Saturdays, pack up and leave town early Sunday morning to perform one last Louisiana show on Sunday in Lake Charles, generally at the Arcade Theater, the Pleasure Pier, the Auditorium, the old Lyric Theater or any of a number of performing venues that operated on Sundays. The Sunday show allowed for another night of receipts in

This image of the local Eureka Brass Band was numbered by a previous owner, but no key to the identities of the persons exists. *Courtesy McNeese University Archives.*

The Arcade Theatre was approached via an arcade through the Miller Building. The facility caught fire and was destroyed in 1985. *Courtesy McNeese University Archives.*

Louisiana, as strict Texas blue laws forbade entertainment on the Sabbath. This arrangement provided for one last paying audience, broke no laws and worked beautifully for both acts and for audiences, at least until the era of talkies and the death of vaudeville. Big musical acts and traveling theater continued the practice of Sunday performances until World War II and, occasionally, even after. Local audiences were able to witness such national performers as Houdini, Isadora Duncan, the St. Louis Symphony and the Barrymores.

While professional traveling troupes provided opportunities for mass entertainment, local house bands made up the gaps at least for live music. For the most part, local musicians were family grown and church inspired. In particular, African American churches focused their worship on both choral and instrumental music. Skills honed in church choirs and orchestras made for great musicianship and a high degree of proficiency. The best example of musical virtuosity is that of the late Nellie Lutcher, who, as a child, was able to successfully fill in at the last minute as a piano player for the great Ma Rainey on one of Rainey's concerts in Lake Charles. Nellie went on to fame as a singer-songwriter in California, recording several jazz and R&B albums, including a duet with Nat King Cole. Nellie even managed the musicians' union in Los Angeles for a time.

A distinctive local sound developed, created as a fusion of cultures and influences. Lake Charles is a salad bowl of Cajuns, creoles, African Americans, relocated upland southerners, Germans and Texans. Instruments were added or changed, melodies were modified, rhythms were altered and musical boundaries were blended and bent. Many early solo artists and local bands performed at roadhouses and dance halls as part of the continuum of coastal south Louisiana music that includes Cajun, zydeco, swamp pop and swing. Local recording companies in Lake

Charles, especially Eddie Schuler's Goldband label, captured this energy and creativity in many early records, some of which found regional if not national fame. And while Eddie claimed he "discovered" Dolly Parton (whose uncle happened to work in Lake Charles for a time and knew Eddie), his greater claim to fame was the documenting and recording of a distinctive new coastal Louisiana set of sounds.

A considerable number of music and entertainment venues were scattered throughout the city, with a fair number clustered along east U.S. Highway 90 and Louisiana Highway 14. These venues went by various names—taverns, bars, honky-tonks, dance halls, restaurants and private clubs—and all of them provided hardworking men (and women) a needed respite or renewal, as the case may be. These sites were popular but little spoken of in polite society, although they were well known to plant operators, airmen at the SAC base, construction workers, longshoremen and even college students. Long the bane of many a Calcasieu preacher or police officer, if not for the open dancing, music and alcohol (even during Prohibition) then for the alleged illegal gambling that was said to be conducted in back rooms, these restaurants, taverns, diners and honky-tonks catered to the men and

This posed image of the so-called Chicken Thief Gang documents one of the elements that gave Battle Row its name. The rough-and-ready lifestyle was part of the "work hard, play harder" ethic of the times. *Courtesy McNeese University Archives.*

women who came to southwest Louisiana to find their fortunes or just to work, beginning in the Great Depression until the 1990s. (Some operate even today, but more discreetly.) Many of these sites are long gone, including the Green Frog, the Aragon, the Bamboo Club, John's Barn, Prejean's, Harry Shay's and Papania's. Their colorful names and even more colorful reputations are now only memories.

To some extent, these roadhouses were just a continuation of what had been the wild and wooly, sometimes combative history of Battle Row, the name attached to Railroad Avenue between Ryan and Enterprise. In the nineteenth and very early twentieth centuries, Battle Row was the preferred convergence point for longshoremen, mill- and rail workers, shipbuilders, shopkeepers, cowboys and farmers on rowdy Friday and Saturday evenings. Newly paid men gathered for drinks, entertainment and a bit of fun at the saloons and sporting houses that lined the street. For at least three generations, Lake Charles mayors and council members campaigned on clearing Battle Row of its rowdies and shutting down its sporting houses, even when at least two of the mayors in question were major—but secret—landlords in the area. The periodic police raids did little to settle the dust. Time itself took the sting out of Battle Row. As merchants and businesses vacated premises to relocate to quieter parts of town, the resulting vacant buildings were no longer rentable—they had been soured by Battle Row's sordid reputation. The once-bustling street lined with buildings from one end to the other is today a mere shell.

In 1939, an eighty-acre site that had been the parish "poor farm" was donated by the police jury (the parish governing body) to LSU for the establishment of a junior college. The site, bounded by Ryan Street on the west and the Gulf Highway on the east, was literally in the country. The intention had been to expand agricultural and practical education with a facility managed by the flagship agricultural school in the state. The WPA designed and erected the first buildings—an auditorium, an agricultural arena and a classroom building. That was the modest start of McNeese State University, perhaps the only institution of higher learning named not for its founder or a major donor, but for an independent educator not associated with the institution.

John McNeese, the first superintendent and a pioneer educator in Calcasieu Parish, had died some twenty-five years before. But so strong was the legacy of McNeese in fostering a culture of support for education in the area that there was no other choice in the naming of this new institution. The establishment and growth of the junior college, later to be a degree-issuing four-year college and then a university, helped to provide a stable anchor to what had been the lonely south end of the city. The faculty, students and staff of the university have played a large role in connecting with the community. In addition to offering a continuing-education program and a very active and well-followed sports program, McNeese offers a season of humanities and arts events called Banners.

One of the principal creations of John McNeese was the establishment of Lake Charles High School in 1890, in what had been the Acadia College building on Enterprise Boulevard. The impressive school had an exceptional list of academic achievements over its long history. The original high school building was replaced with a massive three-story structure in 1928. It spectacularly burned down in 1951. An updated Lake Charles High School was touted as one of the most modern and progressive secondary school facilities in the South. Lake Charles High School continued for almost another forty years, eventually merging with W.O. Boston High under the Lake Charles–Boston High School name. When closed down as an operating high school, the site was converted to an educational enrichment center called the Academy of Learning. However, the traditions of the schools—both Lake Charles and Boston—were lost in practical applications and remain only memories for the alumni. One of the most revered LCHS traditions, the Kiltie precision marching corps, is remembered with a statue and memorial wall in Lock Park.

Lake Charles's long fascination with amateur dramatics can be traced in an unbroken line to the pioneering work of Rosa Hart, who fostered all the arts by making them matter and founded one of the earliest community theaters in America. Rosa (no one called her Miss Hart) was a nonconformist who saw creativity in all she touched. She was educated in New Orleans and is credited with being the very first female cheerleader in America. She was a general cheerleader for Lake Charles her entire life, as well, leading wartime scrap drives and bond sales, tutoring candidates for college and professional schools, operating a popular bookstore and hosting visiting dignitaries. Her experience inspired her to elevate the standards of all the arts—music, dance and drama—and she created the city's first arts organization, the Lake Charles Little Theatre, in 1926. She inspired many of her co-citizens and began a process that encouraged a multitude of other arts groups, performing groups and a professional symphony.

Rosa was responsible for the first desegregated casting of actors on the southern stage, the first radio broadcast of readers' theater for the entertainment of armed forces overseas and the use of professional actors to both teach and perform with amateurs. She may be best known for a publicity coup still discussed today. In 1948, her production of a Louisiana-based play, *The Great Big Doorstep*, was the subject of an eight-page *Life* magazine article that told America there was indeed culture on the bayou. The large theater space in the Lake Charles Civic Center is named for her.

The fascination with amateur dramatics or perhaps just with playacting in general ties into the custom and practice of Mardi Gras, a near-obsessive late winter activity. Originally celebrated in western Europe as the topsy-turvy masked final fling before the privations of Lent, Mardi Gras customs were brought to the New World by the French. The first Mardi Gras celebrations in the Americas were held in Mobile in 1699, although the celebrations in New Orleans are much better known today. In many communities in Louisiana (and in Texas and Alabama to some extent), Mardi Gras is celebrated enthusiastically; an entire season is devoted to events, balls, parades and partying beginning on Twelfth Night on January 6 and ending on Mardi Gras at midnight.

In Lake Charles, the first Mardi Gras celebrations were in the nineteenth century, but the current particular styling of balls, parades and pageants began in earnest in the 1960s. Mardi Gras mayhem is planned by *krewes*, loose associations of individuals who are essentially party planners and socializers. While some krewes do have philanthropic goals, the principal reason to join a krewe is to have a good time and meet new people. The pageantry, partying and parades can be modest and do-it-yourself, or one can hire professionals to provide a wow factor with costumes and effects. For many residents, the crafting and party spirit of Mardi Gras provide a creative outlet, a means to let go and enjoy life. Over seventy krewes operate in the Lake Charles area, and an entire museum at Central School celebrates the glitter, glamor and spice of Mardi Gras.

## Downtown Revisited

In the 1960s and early 1970s, when many American downtowns were slowly disintegrating or actively being torn apart by increased traffic, loss of tenants and competition from new suburbs, Lake Charles made a conscious effort to retain its retail and business center with two grand, but ultimately flawed, urban renewal plans.

In Lake Charles, the traditional downtown was defined as the Ryan Street core, which had served as the primary site for banking, government,

This 1930s view of downtown focuses on the first skyscraper (in all of its ten-story glamor). The Charleston Hotel witnessed many changes downtown. *Courtesy the Imperial Calcasieu Museum.*

retail, hospitality and professional offices for nearly one hundred years. This concentrated center was north–south, paralleling the shoreline. Broad Street is the major east–west street in the area and served as the route for the Old Spanish Trail and later for U.S. Highway 90. In the 1950s, the new interstate highway system right-of-way threaded itself east–west through an entire block—bounded by Church Street on the north and Belden on the south—eventually displacing hundreds of families, splitting up long-established neighborhoods and, in many respects, blocking street flow a mere three blocks from the busy core. The interstate at this point appeared to be designed to move traffic through Lake Charles and not into Lake Charles, a merchant's fear that provoked a strong desire to act.

The first urban renewal plan was to reconfigure all the downtown roadways to what traffic engineers called an efficient grid of one-way streets. The plan actually called for the removal of all vehicular traffic on Ryan Street with the elimination of all front-door parking. The one-way streets were supposed to move more cars to bring in more customers. In a well-meaning but eventually destructive move to keep the rich core of retail on Ryan, the merchants themselves planned this dramatic change to compete with what they perceived as the real coming enemy: enclosed, air-conditioned suburban malls (particularly the 1972-era Prien Lake Mall) and strip-shopping centers mushrooming throughout the city.

Designers of the Ryan Street Mall created an artificial open-air pedestrian mall on what had been two-way traffic and parking lanes. This decades-long experiment on Ryan Street (from Mill Street south to the courthouse) accelerated rather than slowed down the decline of downtown businesses, forced the relocations or closures of dozens of active retail outlets, displaced downtown apartment residents and required the demolition of several landmark structures seen as obsolete. The one-way street grid was tinkered with repeatedly, and for a short time a motorized trolley ferried the rare visitor from outlying parking lots to the increasingly empty Ryan Street Mall. Customers stayed away in droves. Increasingly arcane parking requirements forced demolitions of now-unused parking lots, and the loss of major tenants changed the face of downtown, reducing perhaps 30 percent of it to an empty wasteland. Even today, Ryan Street suffers from the lack of the continuous storefronts that once lined it. Today's empty

The empty Ryan Street Mall, pictured here, was eventually reconverted to vehicular traffic. Surrounding streets were returned to full use, reshaping downtown. *Courtesy McNeese University Archives.*

corners of Ryan Street were once valuable buildings that housed shops, restaurants and offices.

Eventually, "mall improvements" were removed, and Ryan was returned to one-way traffic and then two-way traffic beginning in the late 1980s. Since the beginning of the pedestrian mall concept, Ryan Street had struggled with an ever-diminishing number of customers, a declining tax base, the loss of most professional offices and retail outlets (including the signature department store Muller's in 1985) and the loss of the block-sized Sears store, which eventually reopened in the freshly expanded and revitalized Prien Lake Mall in 1995.

Post–Hurricane Rita (since 2005) improvements include upgrades in utilities, decorative sidewalks and plantings, improved parking and access and a consolidated transit center for city and parish buses. These improvements have encouraged an ongoing and enthusiastic private redevelopment of the street. There is investment in new buildings; new restaurants, shops and gallery ventures in old ones still standing; and a crisply entertaining street life that is beginning to reanimate the traditional downtown. On- and off-street parking, pedestrian-friendly sidewalks, logical signage, landscaping, improved utilities and improved traffic control are the reasons for the renaissance.

The second urban redevelopment project nearly contemporary with the failed urban mall concept was the civic center. That project required the then-defunct working waterfront of Lake Charles to be entirely reconfigured to build the multipurpose Lake Charles Civic Center. The concept was at the time a revolutionary approach to urban redevelopment, at least for most citizens. Rather than building on congested existing land downtown, the grand new civic center was to be constructed on landfill. About eighty acres of water was filled in, eliminating the water's edge for the once-working Front Street (now ironically called Lakeshore Drive). Old warehouses, abandoned ferry landings, disused docking and oil depots were all literally erased to fill in the new land to build the center.

The civic center has not aged well in the view of many. It has a dated-looking and high-maintenance aggregate dash-finish on the exterior. Vaguely International-style but unused elevated walkways circle the building twenty feet in the air, and most people who visit the building enter through a cramped and dark lower-level entry that is covered by the disused walkways. The interior includes much-used meeting rooms with smashing views of the lake (a feature that poses an actual distraction for some events). The facility offers an opera house–sized theater and an eight-thousand-seat arena. The

Post-Rita improvements to the Lake Charles Civic Center property include a reinforced Lakeshore Promenade with date palms and lush landscaping, a well-used marina and various playgrounds with water parks, fountains and benches. *From the author's collection.*

building is surrounded by its park-like Lakeshore Promenade and lots of paved parking.

Unfortunately, the civic center opened too late to save the downtown hotels that were supposed to serve it. Surrounded by acres of free parking, the center now mostly operates as a suburban-style commuter-based public event center that happens to have superb access for outdoor festivals and fairs on a pleasant-looking lake. But with no hotels, retail establishments or restaurants on the civic center grounds, patrons who drive in for events simply drive away afterward, generally leaving the downtown area unvisited and not patronized. Convention and conference planners scheduling for the facility claim to suffer from having no on-site hotel. Other oft-heard complaints include limited break-out rooms, limited audio-visual and computer capacity and limited climate-controlled exhibition space.

According to famed city planner Andres Duany, there is a psychological and physical barrier of parking lot, Lakeshore Drive and a block's worth of structure between the civic center and the restaurants, galleries and shops of Ryan Street. Duany was a consultant in the "Louisiana Speaks" process that helped to galvanize rebuilding efforts after the 2005 hurricane year of Katrina and Rita. He encouraged active redevelopment of the civic center land as part of an ongoing commitment to an expanded, improved and sustainable downtown. Portions of that plan are in place, and improvements have helped to turn the tide somewhat with significant advances in security, traffic flow, utilities, flood control and recreational facilities. Now gracing the civic center landfill are a marina, children's playgrounds and water parks, walking paths and beautifully landscaped Promenade complete with fountains and sculpture. However, private investment on this public land has been squelched for the time being.

The Lake Charles Civic Center continues to benefit from the freedom of wide spaces and free parking. Post-Rita improvements along the water's edge have made the center and its surrounding parks a magnet for large festival-style events that seem to happen every weekend in the spring and fall. However, its full value to downtown Lake Charles remains stymied by a lack of hospitality venues on-site and by the perceived disconnection to the downtown it borders. The civic center, its grounds and features are part of city government and supported by tax revenue and rentals.

As far as Downtown and Lakefront are concerned, there are other, more modest and yet more successful exercises in urban renewal by the city and by the parish government. These efforts include the successful adaptive reuse of existing structures to house the activities of government. The prime example of this good stewardship took place in 1979, when the City of Lake Charles opened a new city hall in what had been an oil-services and business office tower, the Pioneer Building.

The Pioneer Building, constructed in 1948 by oil wildcatters Mordello Vincent and Lee Welch, served for twenty-five years as the southwest Louisiana headquarters for several oil-services and engineering companies. The building was begun in December 1947. Since businesses moved in as floors were ready, there was no "grand opening." The building was completely occupied by July 1949. The local architectural pioneers Dunn and Quinn provided an upbeat, midcentury vibe to the exterior, particularly the east and northern façades, which feature fossilized limestone, green slate and textured buff brick in horizontal bands. The building was the center for the oil business in southwest Louisiana; the top floor was the site of the private Pioneer Club, currently in residence at the Chase Bank building at Broad and Lakeshore.

Built just after the Great Fire of 1910, the 1911 city hall, designed by trophy architects of the era, Favrot and Livaudais, served the city for sixty-

A midcentury vibe can be seen in this image of the north façade of Lake Charles's city hall. Designed by local architects Dunn and Quinn, the Prairie-style building features green slate, fossilized limestone and buff brick. *From the author's collection.*

eight years. In time, the Italianate structure became overcrowded, and its days housing all city government activities were limited. After the 1979 move to the new office tower, the old city hall building was renovated, initially to serve as city court. However, for that purpose, the building was deemed too small and poorly configured for security. In an effort to retain its period look and feel, the building was revamped to serve as a cultural center with scheduled exhibitions in place year-round. It's the site of many downtown-based activities, including concerts, fairs and a weekly farmers' market. It anchors the scenic Public Square and faces the Historic Calcasieu Courthouse, also a Favrot and Livaudais landmark.

The Calcasieu Parish Police Jury (parish government) has also adaptively reused several once-commercial buildings for government and court use, including the former headquarters of Louisiana Savings at 901 Lakeshore Drive, the former Magnolia Life Insurance Building and the former law offices of Scofield, Bergstedt and Gerard on Ryan Street. In each case, the adaptive reuse plans have saved taxpayer money compared to the erection of entirely new structures at that scale. The Parish Government Campus also includes the purpose-built Parish Government Building on Pithon Street at Gill, the Calcasieu Judicial Center, which is the day-to-day working courthouse (located at Lakeshore and Kirby, almost exactly where the stolen courthouse was relocated in 1852) and the majestic Historic Calcasieu Courthouse, the domed centerpiece of Lake Charles's post-fire recovery.

For newcomers to the city, there are always questions about the very visible, abandoned multistory parking garage occupying what appears to be prime lakeshore real estate adjacent to the interstate just east of the Interstate 10 Bridge. The parking garage is the sole remnant of a long, politically tainted, convoluted and colorful history of a hospitality and casino-gaming venture on that site. There were two hotels that preceded the advent of casino gaming on this site: a 1960s Downtowner property and a 1980s Hilton, later Holiday Inn, property, closer to the bend where Lakeshore Drive curves south. These two properties together offered some five hundred rooms as well as restaurants and amenities just off the interstate highway and had served the motoring public long before the state law changed and local option allowed casino and other forms of gaming.

When casino gaming was made legal in Louisiana in the mid-1990s, a company called Players (with ties to Governor Edwin Edwards) obtained one of the coveted riverboat licenses. It opened and operated a very successful riverboat casino at this site using the existing hotels as its base of operations. The company's early success—made possible by the predicted crowds of

Texas gamblers who came from just thirty miles to the west—encouraged Players to expand and to add a second boat. In 1999, Players assets in Lake Charles were bought by casino operator Harrah's, which made significant onshore improvements at the site, including a new reception court, concourse and parking garage, as well as major alterations to the hotels and restaurants. Hurricane Rita seriously damaged the facility. Harrah's made a business decision to sell off what was left of its assets in the Lake Charles market.

The old Hilton/Holiday Inn property was again renovated by new owners and rebranded as the Lakeshore Hotel. The Downtowner, a primitive design in comparison, had been demolished early on to make way for Harrah's grand new improvements. However, in 2008, the serious flood damage to the Lakeshore Hotel from Hurricanes Ike and Gustave was not repairable. The structure was determined to be a total loss, and the entire four-story facility was demolished. The parking garage, apparently built to higher engineering standards, was retained for possible redevelopment.

A westward view of the lake captures the distant arch of the Interstate 10 Bridge in the background and the marina to the right. Even though nearly everything on or near this body of water has been radically changed in the last 150 years, water still provides the focal point for the city. *From the author's collection.*

The now mostly cleared-off land was donated to the city by the new owner, Pinnacle Corporation. This final piece of shoreline may someday be developed if a reasonable means to raise the baseline elevation can be worked out. In a strange twist, the so-called Pinnacle site shares its eastern border with one of the oldest named and occupied locations in the entire region, Bilbo Cemetery, the history of which goes back to the days of Cantonment Atkinson in the nineteenth century.

Another sidelight: Harrah's riverboat licenses had been captured by Pinnacle for a planned casino project in Baton Rouge and for a second Pinnacle property as a companion resort to its successful L'Auberge casino in south Lake Charles. L'Auberge du Lac (as it was termed then) was Pinnacle's upscale investment designed to capture the Texas trade. It opened the year of Rita. L'Auberge was a resounding success from the very start, and a companion resort was viewed as a good business plan. However, a variety of legal maneuvers, market conditions, regulatory red tape and a change in company management induced Pinnacle to abruptly end its quest for a companion resort to the L'Auberge property. That companion resort, to be called Sugarcane Bay, was already in the design and construction prep stages. Pinnacle had to essentially relinquish that final Louisiana casino license. The newly available license was eventually successfully captured by developer Tillman Fertitta for the iconic Golden Nugget property, which now operates next door to L'Auberge. The competing casinos share waterfront on the Calcasieu Ship Channel.

## Lost Landmarks

The nonprofit Calcasieu Historical Preservation Society created and operates two marking programs for historic locations, features and structures. The first, the Calcasieu Landmark program, identifies and marks existing historic properties using a juried nomination and selection process. Begun in 1986, the organization has marked about 120 structures and sites in Calcasieu Parish, with perhaps 90 percent of the marked sites being in Lake Charles. The selected site is identified with a distinctively shaped cypress wood or white marble marker with the site's name and construction date. Research and historic images that formed the nomination are archived at McNeese State University's Frazar Library, and the society's website (www.calcasieupreservation.org) provides online information and access to other resources.

The second marking program is for Lost Landmarks. Begun in 2012, this program identifies and marks the locations of once-important and now entirely lost structures and sites. The custom-cast metal markers provide a thumbnail history of the location to tourists and members of the general public. To date, six Lost Landmark signs have been installed that tell the stories of eleven lost landmarks. More Lost Landmark signs are in the works.

The locations of the markers and the thumbnail histories of the sites are as follows:

## Majestic Hotel (Bilbo at Pujo Street)

This marker, located in the 800 block of Ryan Street, tells the story of the four landmarks that once stood on that block. *From the author's collection.*

On this site stood the Majestic Hotel from 1906 to 1965. Advanced for its day, the Majestic's own water system was used to save it (and surrounding properties) during the Great Lake Charles Fire of 1910. The Majestic Hotel was operated for some time by Emma Michie, who hosted Harry Houdini, the Barrymores, General and Mrs. Eisenhower and Jackie and John Kennedy, among other national figures. The hotel was the center of social, political and cultural life for southwest Louisiana. Deemed obsolete, the hotel was demolished in 1965 for parking.

## The Arcade Theatre and Miller Building, the Paramount and the Weber Building (822 Ryan Street to 840 Ryan Street)

Four important landmarks once stood here, part of an unbroken line of buildings from Railroad Avenue to Clarence Street.

The Weber Building housed professional offices and was the center of Western Union communications for this region. The offices were part of the regionally based Kelly-Weber companies, which included lumber, wholesale trade, agriculture and even maritime shipping. The six-story tower was demolished for parking.

Named for the public passage that connected the working auditorium at the rear of the property to Ryan Street, the Arcade Theatre was the premier venue for concerts, plays, vaudeville and other performances. The stage featured such top-flight acts as Houdini, the St. Louis Symphony and the Barrymores, in addition to many community events.

The passage ran through the Miller Building, a three-story structure that housed offices and shops. In 1978, the entire complex was listed in the National Register; however, a fire gutted the facility beyond salvation in 1985.

Just north of the Miller Building was the Paramount Theater, one of the opulent movie palaces of that chain. The Paramount was the grandest of Lake Charles movie houses, one of over twenty now demolished, which included the Lyric, the Pitt, the Delta, the Ritz and the Palace.

## *Ball's Auditorium (Enterprise Boulevard North at St. John Street)*

One block from this site stood Ball's Auditorium from 1945 to 1995. Here, Reginald Ball Sr. operated a trade school to help returning World War II African American veterans obtain jobs through training in the crafts. By the 1950s, the trade school had largely completed its task, and the facility began to be used extensively for community activities, concerts and paid events. In the 1950s and 1960s, Ball's Auditorium hosted such performers as Otis Redding, Ruth Brown, Fats Domino, Ray Charles, Sam Cooke and James Brown. It was a popular venue on what was then called "the Chitlin' Circuit." After its heyday, the facility gradually deteriorated and saw fewer bookings and uses. What was left was razed.

## *Lost Railroad Stations (Clarence Street at Ryan Street)*

At least four railroad stations were located in Lake Charles, all of which have been lost. On Railroad Avenue at Bilbo were passenger and freight stations (circa 1880) for Louisiana Western Railroad, later Southern Pacific, which ran to points east and west. The Lake Charles and Northern Railroad ran north to DeRidder, Louisiana. The passenger station was lost to fire in 1984, and the freight station was demolished shortly thereafter. The salvaged metal brackets can be seen in the Amtrak Station on Railroad Avenue at Ryan Street.

Kansas City Southern's passenger terminal, built in 1925, was located at the corner of Ryan and Pryce (originally Lawrence) Streets. Kansas City Southern connected north to the main line at DeQuincy, Louisiana. The terminal was demolished in 1989. The 1925 station replaced an earlier Union Station (circa 1894) located at Pryce and Front Street.

This was the site of the Iron Mountain–Missouri Pacific Terminal, circa 1892. The rail line for this station curved south on Common Street and ran east and north to connect to Alexandria and points north. The terminal was demolished in the late 1960s.

## *LaGrange High School (Ryan Street at School Street)*

In 1903, Mesard LaGrange donated an acre for a one-room schoolhouse at this site. In 1913, he offered to donate nine more acres for an expansion of the school. The school board at the time offered him $1,000 for the land to obtain clear title. In 1929, the school opened with two grand brick buildings meeting the needs of students from the entire south part of the parish on this side of the river. A larger LaGrange Senior High School was constructed on Louisiana Avenue in 1954. At that time, the Ryan Street facility became a junior high school. The school was declared obsolete and surplus in 1983. The massive buildings were demolished, and much of the property was returned to commerce. The soccer fields were part of the original school site.

## *Louisiana Baptist Orphanage (Seventh Street at Bank Street)*

Area congregations constructed a two-story orphanage in 1899 that housed up to 150 children at a time. This location was selected for the wholesome, rural character of the setting. The landmark structure was so identified with this part of the community that the entire area came to be known as Baptist Meadows. In 1925, the orphanage closed. The building and grounds were purchased by Mrs. J.A. Landry, who donated the site to the Christian Brothers for a Catholic boys' high school. In 1927, Landry Memorial High was opened. The original orphanage building had been demolished as obsolete by the time Landry was merged with St. Charles Academy and Sacred Heart High in 1970 to form St. Louis Catholic High School.

The Lost Landmark program is ongoing according to representatives of the society. They plan to research and to install one or more markers yearly as they are able and as stories remain to be told. The program is funded privately by the society and with financial project assistance from the Lake Charles and Southwest Louisiana Convention and Visitors Bureau.

## THE NATIONAL REGISTER IN LAKE CHARLES

In all of Calcasieu Parish, there are only 18 current sites (as of 2017) that have merited listing in the National Register of Historic Places, with 12 of them in Lake Charles. For comparison, Orleans Parish (New Orleans) has 164 sites; East Baton Rouge Parish (Baton Rouge) has 87; Caddo Parish (Shreveport) has 68; Lafayette Parish (Lafayette) has 32; Rapides Parish (Alexandria) has 78; and Ouachita Parish (Monroe) has 31. It may truly be observed that, while the history of the area is important and intense, the rush to identify and label its historic resources lags somewhat behind the rest of this history-conscious state.

In Lake Charles are the Calcasieu-Marine National Bank, the Noble Building, the Charleston Hotel (all on Pujo Street), the Calcasieu Courthouse, the Cathedral of the Immaculate Conception and the 1911 City Hall (part of the legacy of recovery from the Great Fire of 1910), Muller's Department Store, the Episcopal Church of the Good Shepherd, McNeese University Auditorium, the Waters-Pierce Stable building, Cash Grocery and Sales and the Lake Charles Historic Charpentier District. Lost to fire after it was listed in the National Register was the Miller Building and Arcade Theater complex. Other listings in the parish include the vintage Iowa High School building and baseball great Ted Lyon's house in Vinton. The Jackson Dogtrot House, the All Saints Chapel and the Kansas City Southern Depot are all in DeQuincy. The Deweyville-Starks Swing Bridge over the Sabine River near Starks is a site shared with the State of Texas.

To have these properties placed in the register, the owners researched and documented the history and consulted with historians to explore the whole story of the structure and its place in the context of historic themes, ideas, movements or important individuals. The owners themselves signed off on the nominations, to be considered first on a statewide basis, then nationally through the Department of the Interior, with the eventual listing in the Congressional Record. In short, a strongly documented case

Calcasieu Marine National Bank is individually listed in the National Register of Historic Places. A product of Favrot and Livaudais, the bank building today is not much altered from this 1930s view. *Courtesy the Imperial Calcasieu Museum.*

has to be made why any particular building or site is especially important and deserving of recognition. Every nomination begins locally. Each case is reviewed by the Office of Historic Preservation staff, by other historians, by a panel of experts in various fields at the state level and, finally, by the secretary of the interior in Washington, who ratifies the nomination.

For National Register historic districts like the Lake Charles Historic District, locally referred to as the Charpentier Historic District, proposed boundaries are suggested and a building-by-building survey and description is undertaken relatively early on. While the survey lists structures as "contributing" or "non-contributing" to the developing district, once approved by the local governing authority, all the structures in the district are protected, if so designated by guidelines and ordinance. In some cases, historic districts can be created that are locally recognized (and perhaps afforded local protection by ordinance). That is the case with Margaret Place, a city-recognized historic district but not yet a National Register property. In Lake Charles, a Historic Preservation Commission serves as part of city planning and zoning and provides public review of modifications and changes to structures.

Many communities have historic districts that are true walkable neighborhoods with high percentages of longtime residents and enthusiastic newcomers. In many historic districts, residents benefit from well-cared-for homes and mature plantings. Visitors are charmed by the streetscapes. These districts form a sizable portion of the cultural tourism attractions all over America.

Historic districts do not have to be large. In fact, most historic districts in America, whether locally recognized or in the National Register, are small, sometimes just a block or two. Large districts can have many types of properties—commercial, residential, industrial—with different individual histories, designs and themes. But most historic districts are relatively modest in size. Many smaller districts are recognized for properties closely related by age, style, theme, historic use and proximity.

The local sawmill industry and the practice of carpenter-builders using pattern books connects the properties of the Charpentier District. Here is a current view of the Nason Mansion, one of its most photographed houses. *From the author's collection.*

The district must have original material; authentic and intact styles; and documented connections to social, cultural, educational, commercial, architectural, military or other broad themes. In addition, a property or district may show solid connections to important individuals, events or movements that shaped history on a local, state or national level.

It is wise to develop a well-researched case if you plan to pursue the listing of a single particular house or structure. If planning to petition for a historic district using individual house histories, a good strategy is to involve as many property owners as possible for a "buy-in" to the process and the reasons for doing so. While researching one house may be completed relatively easily if resources are right, creating a district is both an extended research project and a political process and can literally take years. Part of the concern is the perceived loss of control of personal property, which, in these contentious days, can be real.

Professional monitoring and public review of proposed changes to structures and features protects neighboring property values. This is a good argument for promoting historic districts. In pitching for historic districts, a good argument to review is that maintaining and publicly reviewing change of such a district protects value. Not only does a shared architectural heritage provide an economic resource to the community in terms of retained property values, but it also provides an identity and community focus, a potential for cultural tourism and generous aesthetic and quality-of-life benefits. In many coastal communities in the South, the historic areas of town are built on the highest and most sustainable land, offering additional value to existing structures and making the need for careful review of development even more pressing.

Even in conservative and prudent Lake Charles, the Charpentier Historic District took well over a decade to be created from the point of first citizen input, through the surveys and public hearings to the eventual final listing in the Congressional Record in 1990. Proposals have been stymied for decades to develop other districts in Lake Charles, particularly one to protect the very rare and prestigious Shell Beach Road properties, a grandly picturesque series of spectacular mansions, many with beautiful gardens and working boathouses.

The ease with which the modern environment can be and is changed has placed the physical elements of history, buildings, roadways, landscape features, sometimes even the waterways and topography itself, at risk of irrevocable loss. Without them, history can become just words and images on pages and computer screens. Without the physical reminders of what came before, reminders that engage thought and inspire action, history loses its educational edge and becomes just dry facts and dates. If *Lost Lake Charles* has helped to enrich those dry facts and dates or has helped to expand the whole story of this unique region, it has served a noble cause.

Appendix

# HOW TO DISCOVER HISTORY ON YOUR DOORSTEP

*Researching Your Place in History*

For some people, a house is just a house, walls and roof for protection, a box to live in. But for others, it can be much more. A house should be a home, a sanctuary, a refuge from modern life, an expression of lifestyle and a vehicle for social interaction. Particularly for older properties, houses can be much more than architecture for living. They are repositories and catalysts of memory, they can connect families and they record changes in society. By researching one's own house, the process becomes a catalyst to better understanding one's community, or at least to help strengthen a sense of place and belonging.

For some, the interest in local history research begins when buying, inheriting or otherwise acquiring a house in what appears to be an older neighborhood. Older homes are an alternative to living in cookie-cutter subdivisions or in apartments. While there are many sound arguments for living in newly built properties, there will always be an allure in living in older neighborhoods. Many older neighborhoods are closer to the established infrastructure and include long-term residents and well-established patterns. Many older neighborhoods include such practical things as streets with sidewalks, complete utilities, mature plantings, parks and relatively easy access to markets, hospitals, schools, jobs, entertainment and recreation.

For people purchasing homes, real estate listings will be the first source of information about a potential home. Agents are obligated to inform potential owners, banks and financial agents about the estimated age of a house and its history. A buyer should, however, take all information with

# Appendix

a grain of salt and try to get more than just one version of a home's real estate history.

An abstract of title (in Louisiana, at least) can be a helpful document in getting the process started. However, abstracts deal primarily in the history of land, and improvements may or may not be specifically and clearly listed. Here are a few pointers when reading an abstract of title. Try to develop a timeline for your house. Since abstracts focus on land ownership, sort through the line of ownership and through the line(s) of succession. Watch for sudden changes in value. For example, a property that sold in 1899 for $24 suddenly selling in 1900 for $800 may indicate that improvements were made—perhaps a house or other building was constructed on the site. Before concluding that your Victorian country farmhouse was constructed in 1899, fit that information into the setting of what was going on in the larger community to provide a context for interpretation—that $800 sale might have been a barn!

If you purchase a property in Lake Charles, remember that many abstracts in Calcasieu Parish begin with "on the 23rd of April in 1910 a conflagration destroyed many records held in the Calcasieu Parish Courthouse." The abstract goes on to say that a number of sources may have been used to reconstruct records, including testimony from neighbors, independent abstractors, bankers, lawyers and realtors. These "recollections" sometimes give incomplete or even conflicting information, particularly when anecdotal.

Family genealogical sources and courthouse records can be overwhelming and sometimes murky, repetitive and frustrating. The search for paid mortgages, tax records and successions can be spun out to consume lots of time and energy, oftentimes without satisfactory results for amateurs. However, there can be those eureka moments—enthusiastic shouts of "I found it!" heard in courthouse stacks or in libraries and archives. The chase through already archived materials in local libraries and some museums can be very useful.

Luckily, at least here in Calcasieu Parish, there are published versions of house histories for some properties in Lake Charles. There are house history books by the late Lloyd Barras and by the late Nola Mae Ross, to name two popular regional authors. While some of their materials are out of print, copies are retained at the Southwest Louisiana Historical Library in the Carnegie facility downtown. Most parts of Louisiana and the rest of the South have similar popular histories of homes and properties. In some areas, these histories are extensive; in New Orleans, Charleston and Savannah, they are almost exhaustive. Public and regional libraries, property tax offices

# Appendix

and some abstract and title companies can provide amazing information about the chain of ownership.

Website resources can be useful once you obtain a chain of ownership of property. There is quite a bit of history available using various Internet search engines. The address of the property and the names of previous owners can send you on a wild ride of exploration, but be careful not to pin your hopes on just an Internet search. Much detailed history has not yet been converted into electronic format—there is still quite of bit of our history to be digitized and digested.

Some public libraries focus on a community's past and serve as great general resources with lots of tools to uncover local history. Useful are Sanborn maps, which show the physical outline of structures on an engineer's plat for insurance purposes. Helpful, too, are ancient city directories and guides. Family and church histories, as well as cemetery censuses, organizational minutes and records, are useful tools to putting together the historical record about your historic property and the people who lived there. And, consider sharing your information needs with research staff at the resource libraries. Generally, they are very cooperative and clever at directing you to other resources and to newly uncovered research being conducted by others.

Formal archives are also available at many college and university libraries, and there is the Historic New Orleans Collection and similar collections in other cities. For properties with extensive histories, you may need to review materials at the offices of the secretary of state, the official state archives or private museum collections. Even with these additional resources, remember that local information is best regarding local properties; local physical searches are almost always the best way to start.

In many areas, oral history, particularly from longtime residents of the neighborhood, can be useful in helping to gather information, particularly for names and interests of individuals involved with particular sites. A comment, for example, that a former resident was a Mason or a veteran opens up new avenues of research. It helps, of course, to have long-established residents who enjoy talking about what they remember about the past.

Some individuals have found success using newspapers and local journals, either online or in print form. For example, Lake Charles has an impressive online archive of the *American Press* newspaper and its predecessor papers dating to 1898. One way to begin a newspaper search using online news archives is to type in the street address, the name of the builder and a previous owner or resident of the property in question. Be prepared to repeat as necessary.

## Appendix

In a practical sort of way, an actual architectural house survey essentially "deconstructs" the house in terms of style, materials used, comparisons to other houses possessing similar features and layout. Architects, experienced craftsmen or trained draftsmen can be helpful in this. They can sometimes identify original building materials, note additions and renovations and compare the actual structure with other structures on a local and, perhaps, regional level. Old photographs can be helpful in establishing what the structure looked like earlier and to establish if porches, fireplaces, siding, windows and other features date to the original construction or have been added at some subsequent point.

House surveys, particularly when you factor in styles and materials, can be complex things, but they can be useful in determining history and context for an individual house. They can also determine alterations, renovations and lost features and can sometimes suggest what is original and authentic.

However, validate your findings with other sources—don't assume. Architectural taste and historical styling, particularly in southwest Louisiana, can be very eclectic and contrary to strict architectural rules. What may seem bizarre to a scholar or architectural historian may just be a quirky historic house, especially here in Lake Charles and other towns in southwest Louisiana. A case in point in Lake Charles is the Christman House at Pujo and Bank Streets. It is practically at the epicenter of the Charpentier District and is in the local Calcasieu Landmark Register. Its unusual porch railings—two simple round batons connecting with fluted columns and having no balusters—were originally viewed by the consulting historical architect as not being authentic to the house, with an observation that, surely, the simple turned cylinders of wood were additions, perhaps from the 1950s. It took an ancient tintype from the owner's own collection of family pictures to show that the railings looked the same way they do now as on the day the house was built.

Similarly, the consulting architectural historians deduced that most of the houses in the Lake Charles Charpentier District were built by carpenters using plan books and visual descriptions rather than by using formal architectural blueprints. In doing this, the owners or the carpenters chose to vary what they built and how they built to suit the house's particular site or the owner's taste. Many of what were supposed to be formal Greek Revival houses (which academically have even numbers of columns with strictly symmetrical façades) were constructed with odd numbers of columns. Houses with odd numbers of columns are seen all over the Charpentier District in Lake Charles and in other parts of southwest Louisiana, as

# Appendix

Research shows that odd numbers of columns—when you expect even numbers—can be a standard for the area. Houses with five, three and even seven columns are common in Lake Charles, like this example on Pujo Street. *From the author's collection.*

well. It's a recognized local quirk that newcomers might wonder about. To honor the mostly French-speaking carpenters, the local name for the district "Charpentier" is the French word for "carpenter."

Once a homeowner has sorted through the historic clutter and establishes a specific house timeline and history, the researcher can begin to relate that house history to the history of the area in general. In other words, a history can lead to establishing a bit of context and connect the house to area themes, trends, movements or individuals with their own colorful histories.

Once you have a history and a context for your property, you may want to look at having the history formally acknowledged and recorded. In many parts of the country, local historical societies or associations maintain landmark registers, and some local governments recognize historic sites. In Calcasieu Parish, the Calcasieu Historical Preservation Society (CHPS) maintains a formal parish-wide landmark registry that annually recognizes and marks properties and maintains archives of researched house materials along with images and histories. The markers and online histories are prestigious and sought after. The signage and online information enhances and forms a basis for cultural tourism and provides the area with an improved sense of place and quality of life. Even if your own community does not offer a formal marking system, you can, on your own, depending on finances and personal taste, create a marker and document your own home. House scrapbooks, like baby books, can become family heirlooms.

The CHPS listings in Calcasieu Parish are recognized as significant and are cited by the state preservation office as one of the best and most complete local registries of its kind in the South. Properties in the register are identified with a distinctive sign naming the structure and construction date, and many are referred to in current brochures and guides published by the Lake Charles and Southwest Louisiana Convention and Visitors' Bureau for the benefit of cultural tourists and general visitors to the area. Historic sites in Lake Charles even have a Convention and Visitors' Bureau smart-phone app routing tool with GPS coordinates that provides touring information, property history and links to resources for visitors and locals who want an instant history lesson.

There is no state-level registry in Louisiana as there are in other states, so the only other formal recognition a property owner might want to pursue is that of the very prestigious and select National Register of Historic Places, which is overseen by the secretary of the interior. In Louisiana, inquiry and application to the National Register begins by contacting the Department of Culture, Recreation and Tourism (CRT), Office of Historic Preservation. Check for the process in your own state.

# BIBLIOGRAPHY

Barras, Lloyd. *Early Homes of Lake Charles*. Baton Rouge, LA: Claitor's Publishing Division, 1975.

Benoit, Robert. *Imperial Calcasieu*. Charleston, SC: Arcadia Publishing, 2000.

Davis, Edwin Adams. *Louisiana: A Narrative History*. Baton Rouge, LA: Claitor's Publishing, 1971.

Davis, Edwin Adams, and Joe Gray Taylor. *Louisiana: The Pelican State*. Baton Rouge: Louisiana State University Press, 1975.

Hennick, Louis C., and E. Harper Charlton. *Louisiana: Its Street and Interurban Railways*. Shreveport, LA: Journal Printing, 1962.

Ross, Nola Mae Wittler. *Airplanes for Breakfast*. N.P.: printed by author. 2000.

———. *Crimes of the Past*. N.p.: printed by author, 2004.

———. *Diaries of Louisiana Circuit Riders*. N.p.: printed by author, 2006.

———. *Jean Lafitte: Louisiana Buccaneer*. N.p.: printed by author, 1990.

———. *Krause and Managan Lumber*. N.p.: printed by author, 2002.

# Bibliography

———. *Mardi Gras in Calcasieu Parish*. N.p.: printed by author, 1991.

———. *Pioneers of Calcasieu Parish*. N.p.: printed by author, 1988.

———. *Veterans Remember: A 50$^{th}$ Anniversary*. N.p.: printed by author, 1995.

Williams, T. Harry, Richard N. Current and Frank Freidel. *American History: A Survey*. New York: Alfred A. Knopf, 1963.

———. *A History of the United States to 1877*. New York: Alfred A. Knopf, 1964.

Watson, Thomas. *Early Exploration and Settlement of the Lower Calcasieu Watershed*. Transcribed by Lenora White. Lake Charles, LA: McNeese State University Archives and Special Collections. Lake Charles, Louisiana, 2008.

# INDEX

## A

abstract  83, 132
abstract of title  132
Acadians  32, 33, 34, 35
Adams-Onis Treaty  32
African Americans  21, 108, 123
American Press  78, 79, 133
American Revolution  30
amethyst brooch  37
Attakapas  27, 29

## B

Baptist Meadows  16, 124
Barbe High School  18
Battle Row  61, 110
Bilbo Cemetery  33, 46, 121
Borden's  69
*Borealis Rex*  57, 59
Brimstone Mines  95
Broadmoor  18
Broad Street  16, 18, 43, 51, 60, 66, 91, 113, 117

## C

Calcasieu Historical Preservation Society  121, 135
Calcasieu Lake (Big Lake)  22, 29
Calcasieu longleaf pine  41
Calcasieu River  14, 17, 22, 29, 35, 39, 41, 42, 43, 53, 68, 96, 97, 98, 107
Campeche  38
Cantonment Atkinson  32, 121
carpetbaggers  22, 48, 49
casino gaming  119
Catholics  46, 90
Central School  75, 90, 112
Charpentier Historic District  16, 19, 53, 125, 126, 128, 134
Chennault, Claire  92, 93
Chitimacha  27, 28
Cities Services  95
City Docks  19, 38, 97
city hall  71, 76, 77, 83, 88, 89, 117, 119, 125
Civil War  21, 43, 46, 47, 49, 54, 59

# Index

Claiborne, William C.C. 37
commission form 86
CONOCO 95
Contraband Bayou 17, 38, 107
cowboys 35, 93, 110
Creoles 21, 31, 33, 35, 108
cypress 12, 16, 41, 42, 50, 51, 53, 73, 75, 82, 83, 98, 121

## D

Dan (steamboat) 42, 47, 57, 96
Deesport 17
Downtown Development Authority (DDA) 16
Downtown/Lakefront 15, 16
Duany, Andres 116
Dummy-line 60, 66
Dunn and Quinn 117

## E

Edgemont 16

## F

Favrot and Livaudais 45, 87, 89, 90, 117, 119
Fisherville 17
French 27, 29, 30, 33, 44, 112

## G

Galveston 36, 38, 42, 51
Germans 21, 41, 108
Gerstner Air Field 92, 93
Golden Nugget 121
Goos, Daniel 41, 43
Goosport 17, 41, 42, 60, 62, 77

Gordon Drug Store 71, 72, 81
Graywood 19, 104, 105, 106
Greinwich Terrace 18
Greinwich Village 18
Guth Dairy 69

## H

Hart, Rosa 111
Hazel 12, 57, 59
Historic Calcasieu Courthouse 45, 119
Hurricane Rita 16, 18, 19, 64, 115, 117, 120, 121

## I

Immaculate Conception 90, 125
Interstate 10 33, 46
Ishak 27, 28, 29

## K

Kansas City Southern 56, 124, 125
Kelly-Weber (company) 70, 122
Knapp, Seamon K. 67, 68
krewes 112

## L

Lafitte, Jean 32, 36, 37, 38
LaGrange High School 18, 124
Lake Charles Civic Center 98, 112, 115, 116, 117
Lake Charles Little Theatre 111
Lake Charles Memorial Hospital 105
L'Auberge 121
LeBleu, Arsene 37

# Index

LeBleu, Bartheleme  33, 37
letters of marque  36
Louisiana Baptist Orphanage  16, 91, 124
Louisiana Purchase  30, 31, 32, 44
Louisiana Savings  119
Louisiana Speaks  117

## M

Majestic Hotel  51, 73, 81, 82, 122
Mardi Gras  112
Margaret Place  16, 54, 62, 90, 91, 127
Marion  35, 44, 46
marshes  21, 23, 41, 44, 54, 55, 67, 96, 106
Mathieson Alkali  99
McNeese, John  80, 110, 111
McNeese State University  110, 121
McNeese, Susan Bilbo  80
Mermentau River  32
Michigan Men  21, 48, 50, 51, 66, 69
midden  29
midwesterners  22, 55, 64, 66, 69, 70
Mississippi River  30, 31, 33, 36, 54, 57
Missouri Pacific  55, 124
Muller, Julie  69
Muller's  70, 115, 125

## N

Napoleon  30
Natchez  27, 28, 29
Natchitoches  13, 29, 31
National Register of Historic Places  16, 70, 90, 123, 125, 126, 127, 136
New Orleans  30, 31, 32, 34, 35, 36, 38, 49, 51, 54, 69, 75, 87, 107, 111, 112, 125, 132
No Man's Land  31, 32, 35

## O

Oak Park  16, 104, 105
Old Spanish Trail  29, 59, 113
Opelousas  29, 35, 44, 54
Orange Grove Cemetery  78

## P

petrochemicals  13, 22, 56, 95, 97, 99
Pinnacle Corporation  121
Pioneer Building  72, 117
pirates  35, 36, 38
Pithon, Michel de  33, 37
plantation society  47
Pleasure Pier  62, 78, 107
Port of Lake Charles  22, 38, 59, 97, 99
postes  29
prairie  21, 23, 29, 34, 35, 37, 41, 44, 54, 64, 67, 91, 93, 96, 104
Prien Lake Road  18, 72, 103

## R

Railroad Avenue  18, 55, 59, 61, 76, 83, 110, 122, 123
Ramsay, William  50, 51
Red River  31, 32, 33, 47

# INDEX

rice  13, 23, 56, 67, 68, 76, 83, 93, 97, 100
Ryan, Jacob  39, 41, 43, 44
Ryan Street  16, 18, 59, 61, 64, 66, 69, 70, 72, 77, 79, 81, 82, 88, 89, 103, 110, 112, 113, 114, 115, 117, 119, 123, 124
Ryan Street Mall  114

## S

Sabine River  27, 32, 95, 96, 97, 125
Sallier, Catherine LeBleu  37, 38
Sallier, Charles  37, 38
Sallier Oak  37
sawmills  12, 15, 17, 41, 43, 50, 53, 73, 77, 79, 86, 87, 95, 100
schooners  12, 41, 42, 51, 57, 96, 97, 98
Shell Beach Road  59, 83, 128
Southern Pacific  54, 55, 123
south Lake Charles  18, 70, 106, 121
SOWELA  93
Spanish  21, 27, 29, 30, 31, 33, 34, 36
St. Charles Academy  90, 124
steamers  96
St. Landry Parish  44, 84
St. Patrick's sanitarium  75
streetcars  12, 59, 60, 61, 62, 63, 64, 71, 75, 78, 81, 86, 91
sulfur  13, 23, 56, 95, 96
Swift (company)  68, 69, 101

## T

Teche  31, 32, 33, 34, 47, 54
timber  23, 41, 51, 53, 70, 95

## W

Walnut Grove  19, 62, 78
War of 1812  21, 32, 36
Watkins, Jabez Bunting (J.B.)  55, 64, 66, 69
Watkins (rail line)  55, 60
Williams Opera House  73, 78
World War I  92
World War II  19, 59, 93, 95, 99, 108, 123

# ABOUT THE AUTHOR

Adley Cormier has researched Louisiana his entire adult life to gain a unique insight of the culture and history of the region. A native of Breaux Bridge and a history graduate of LSU, he has written multiple monographs and articles for journals and magazines. He has appeared on national television, on Louisiana Public Broadcasting and in independent productions to share the area's unique heritage and culture. He completed a new history of southwest Louisiana for the Chamber Southwest in 2016 and still guides tour groups and journalists. Retired from the Department of Labor, he and his wife, Melinda Antoon Cormier, live in Lake Charles.

*Visit us at*
www.historypress.net

*This title is also available as an e-book*